Dr. Thomas Hoffmann

My Visit to a Better World

A Fateful Train Journey

Translated by: Hilary Teske

Novel

JW hite
Julia

At some places in this book you find the following symbols

☞ **i**

followed by a page number.
They are references to explanations or sources and in-depth information.

Julia White Publishing
Internet: www.julia-white.com

ISBN 978-3934402-77-5

Contents

My visit to a better world

"Is this seat free?"

"Yes, of course."

A friendly gentleman aged about 40 makes room for me. I heave my suitcase on to the luggage rack and drop into the free seat.

Thank goodness! After that day it would have been too much to have to stand during the whole journey! That tax auditor had really finished me off. She wanted to see everything and know everything. I actually had to disclose my entire life to a complete stranger and felt her malevolence, watching how she could catch me out when I was in the trap and where she could strike and cash in. It was awful to be at someone's mercy like that – such powerlessness and humiliation at the same time!

But now I was travelling into the weekend and hopefully would soon take my mind off it.

I am sitting at a table for four, all the seats around me are occupied and some passengers are even still looking for seats. Opposite me are sitting a man and a middle-aged woman, who are clearly travelling together. He is reading a newspaper, she a magazine, and they frequently make brief remarks to one another.

I can read the headline on the front page and of course it is about the euro crisis or the great initiatives to resolve this crisis. For weeks the media have been talking and writing about hardly anything else: everything overcome, everything solved, bail-out schemes, bail-out funds, bla, bla, bla. I can't stand hearing it any longer. Anyway hardly anyone believes all that anymore as the picture on the streets, when you talk to people, tells a completely different story. People have problems, they are not doing well, many are afraid.

The tax auditor as well had revealed in a few remarks today that she had the strictest order to scrape together as much as in any way possible for the government. We are all to be milked down to the last drop so as to be able to delay the collapse of our financial system as far as possible.

I look out of the window. We are just passing through a small de-

serted station. It always pains me to see the dilapidated station buildings and abandoned sidings. We have one of the most extensive rail
networks in the world and are reducing it instead of using it! Since
everything has been seen solely from the view of maximising profit,
so many small places can no longer be reached by train, particularly in the local areas there are fewer and fewer trains, the tickets
are increasingly expensive and the trains have too few seats, like this
evening, although it can be foreseen that on Friday evening a lot of
people will be going away. At the same time, our roads are cracking
more and more under the load of trucks, the pollution from noise and
exhaust fumes from road traffic is increasing and a growing number of
new roads have to be constructed. It is quite obvious that there is no
higher level plan with the public good in mind.

MO: Just look at that!

the man opposite me suddenly says to the woman, and these words
wake me from the light sleep I must have fallen into.

MO: The next vaccination campaign must be coming.

He points to an article I unfortunately cannot see. The woman takes
a brief look at it and replies in a cynical undertone:

WO: Oh no! And here they reported …

She closes the magazine so as to have a look at the front page.

☞ p. 182 WO: … two weeks ago that the WHO wants to eradicate measles this
year. What a coincidence!

My neighbour intervenes:

N: Are you talking about the outbreak of measles in Berlin?

MO: Yes, they are making such a to-do about it that you don't know
      what to believe anymore! Every year there is at least one piece
      of bad news about an epidemic so that people obediently have
      themselves vaccinated.

WO: And in the end it all fizzles out.
      What happened to swine flu? Or avian flu? Or Ebola? In the end
      a lot of the vaccines purchased at great expense even had to be
      destroyed because the population didn't want to be vaccinated.

She is visibly agitated.

WO: They always make the vaccinations out to be an unproblematic, risk-free solution or even the only possible remedy. But in the end it is only about money.

MO: Yes, the vaccine manufacturers undoubtedly have the greatest benefit. They are also in close contact with politicians.

WO: You know, I'm an alternative practitioner. I know what I'm talking about. Vaccinations are anything but unproblematic. I have to do with a large number of people suffering from long-term and even irreparable damage from vaccinations. And that's no wonder either, with all the problem substances vaccines contain. However, a large part of the population is not even aware that their problems have to do with vaccinations.

i
p. 139

N: But more and more people are becoming aware of that and are critical of vaccinations.

WO: There would be even more of them if the media reported on the problems. But the normal person hardly learns anything about them. Even doctors don't seem to be aware of the problems – or at least pretend not to be. That is all deliberately staged to guarantee the pharmaceutical industry's earnings. That's why the bread is taken directly from the mouths of naturopathic practitioners. As a therapist I have to be constantly on the watch not to violate some regulation or a new EU directive. Certain compounds are almost unavailable now, even well-tried household remedies! Anything that is not proved by a scientific study is not allowed to be recommended anymore and is used less and less, even when it has proved itself over centuries.

I: But excuse me,

I chip in.

I: Surely it is only sensible that the remedies which are allowed to be used are first of all examined objectively and scientifically.

WO: If science and scientists were objective! I really wish we had a large independent research institution to examine all these controversial issues and clarify them once and for all. Instead, a large part of the scientific studies in the medical sector is commissioned or at least funded by the pharmaceutical industry. And they don't do it to obtain results which harm their own products!

I: So you think they cheat?

WO: Maybe not directly, although some cases of obvious cheating have been uncovered. But here it's mostly not a question of processes that can be evaluated clearly and objectively as "black" or "white" as in physics. There's almost always room for subjective interpretation: is such a borderline case rated as sick or still as healthy – or perhaps as invalid because it doesn't fit into the concept? Where is the boundary line for the measurements? Which symptoms do I consider and in which weighting? How generous am I in my choice of test persons? How many test persons do I take? Alone such elastic concepts can influence the results enormously.
And there's further room to manoeuvre in the presentation of the study. Which risks do I mention and which do I leave out? How detailed is the bibliography? Does it also include critical or negative literature?

N: You also have to put yourself in the position of the scientists concerned. They are either employed directly by the pharmaceutical company or work at a university and know that their salaries are being paid by the firm during the study. Do you think they deliver results which are disadvantageous for the firm?

I: Yes, of course. But why does that influence the results of the research?

N: Not only the results but the entire research. First of all, it depends from the start on which issues are to be examined at all. Such a scientist – who, let's say, has vested interests – won't conduct a wide-ranging study into the side-effects and risks of the product of the firm commissioning the study or make a comparison with a better product from their competitor or about the positive impact of particular plants or life and dietary habits which do not create sales. Finally, at the end of the study they can decide entirely subjectively whether it is to be published or not. And it often happens that studies with undesired results are simply not published. Everyone can judge for themselves whether that's to be seen as cheating or not.

As far as the results are concerned, we mustn't forget that we are mainly dealing with statistical evaluations of the history of diseases here. Those are simply not objective facts, as the subjective aspect of the patients and also of those treating them play a very important role.

I: And that also determines health or sickness?

N: According to ancient – and also completely modern – findings, the most important factor for sickness and health lies in the mental area. That's why observed blinded studies and double blind controlled studies were introduced and made the standard so that neither the patient nor the person treating them know if they're being treated with the actual active ingredient or a placebo. In ☞ threefold blind controlled studies not even the person evaluating p. 181 the trial who's compiling the statistics from the study knows. The critical scientists are aware of possible weak points. That's why a standard has been introduced for medical publications that a statement about conflicting interests has to be made at the end.

I: Well, everything is in order then! What's all the fuss about?

N: Well, such a standard was introduced because there was an existing – and entrenched – deficiency. That this immediately ceases and alternative ways are simply not sought is contrary to all experience and very doubtful. The statement on conflicting interests, for instance, is created by clicking four times in an online form. It's doubtful whether – and how – that is controlled.
Besides that, most scientists – even critical ones – unfortunately forget that they do in fact have to apply their findings to themselves.

I: What do you mean?

N: Almost 100 years ago modern physics found out that in quantum mechanics the subject of an experiment and the experimenter, i.e. object and subject, can't in principle be separated at all, but "objective" results are more than ever considered to be the only valid criterium everywhere today.

WO: And that of all things in medicine, where we have to do with the human being, a highly complex, multi-level, multi-dimensional being. That's why homeopathy has been as good as ignored in scientific research up to today because of this delusional striving for objectivity.

And so we've got back to the current status quo – new standards or not – where no ingredients or fields or applications are allowed to be indicated in the package insert for homeopathic remedies, on the grounds that they aren't scientific! Every the therapists don't get anything more from the manufacturer. So it's getting more and more difficult to treat patients competently with home-opathy. Actually it's obvious that the government isn't interested in people's health at all!

N: The government probably can't do what they would like either. They also get their guidelines from higher up.

WO: What do you mean by that?

N: Well, for instance, today a lot of directives come from the EU Commission in Brussels. You've just said that yourself. The na-tional governments simply have to implement these directives. And the EU Commission isn't a democratic institution. None of us elected them.

I: Well, ...

I chime in,

I: ... maybe not directly.

But the Commission is filled by the individual governments, so that's a democratic process.

My neighbour smiles and starts speaking in a grave voice:

N: Isn't it just fantastic what you elect with a single vote – the mem-bers of parliament, the Chancellor and the government and even the EU Commission! All with just one vote!

But actually you're only electing a party, which then fills all the other positions in a more or less in-party process. That can't be described as democratic. In a democracy the people should actu-ally govern and not give up their right of participation in the form of a blanket vote.

I: Seen in that way, you're absolutely right but how else do you want to organise it? You have to have representatives who vote on the actual issues.

N: You don't have to but it is sensible for reasons of practicality. Only there's a big difference if you know the representatives or have access to them or not. You're sure to know some members of the local council. And when you have a concern they're the people to contact on the spot. Now just imagine the local council sends a representative to a higher council. This representative isn't far away and has a direct connection to the local council.
Then imagine that this representative is bound by the instructions of the local council. Then they can only vote in accordance with what the local council and ultimately the community has decided.

I: What you say is interesting. In that model every vote is virtually brought down to the local level indirectly.

N: Yes, it is.

My neighbour nods.

N: The local council decides how its member should vote. And so the local council can bring the community's opinion into every single point to be voted on. And, in turn, each citizen can make their opinion heard in the local council. In this way you have a form of democracy rather in which representatives vote but finally each community or municipality is asked via its local council.

MO: What a difference to our present system! Today every member of parliament has to decide for the most part as their party prescribes – no matter what their voters would like.

N: If they've been directly elected to a constituency at all! Half of them are simply delegated by their party. And the strongest party appoints the Chancellor and the ministers and then the commissioner in the EU Commission as well.

WO: That brings us back to the people who determine today's politics,

the alternative practitioner pipes up again.

N: Not entirely. Although they determine our governments, they are still not really the ones who decide. They also get their orders from above.

WO: Who from?

The man next to me hesitates a moment. Then he answers:

N: We hardly know the real decision-makers. But they have the most effective instrument to convince and influence others – money.

WO: Oh, you mean the banks!

she retorts in a slightly disappointed tone.

N: No, the owners of the banks, the high finance clans. They govern the banks and hence politics.

MO: Oh God! That's just some kind of hackneyed conspiracy theory,

says the man opposite me dismissively.

N: You think so? But I don't actually want to discuss that. It's a fact that because of their debts all countries are dependent today on private lenders, the nicely termed "markets." What lengths they go to so as not to fall from the grace of these lenders, for instance be downgraded by rating agencies! Don't you think that alone the financial dependency of a country on private banks is an alarming encroachment on its sovereignty?

MO: Yes, of course, I don't want to question that. I only resist the idea of some greedy bankers forcing our politicians to do something at gunpoint.

N: They don't need to do anything like that. Alone the established rules of this financial system automatically play into their hands.

MO: What do you mean by that?

N: Well, you maybe know this little mathematical puzzle: If someone had lent one dollar at a 6% interest rate in 1800, how much would it be today?

MO: Yes, I know it. So how much would it be?

N: Over 275,000 dollars!

I: Ooh, very lucrative!

I say laughing.

I: My great-great-grandpa should have done that!

N: Yes,

replied the man next to me in a reflective tone.

N: That's the view of most people: lending or investing money is very worthwhile; you don't have to do anything and just let the money work for you …
But have you ever thought what it means that because of this simple procedure of lending a dollar such a huge sum has to be generated to repay the debt with interest and compound interest? If you repay those 275,000 dollars, you haven't had any benefit – apart from just being able to make use of this one dollar for over 200 years.
Normally you buy something tangible when you spend money – either material or a service. But in this case you don't get anything tangible or any saving which would be fitting with this sum in any way. Nothing of value is created for anybody.

MO: But I did get a service. The dollar was still available to me for 200 years and I was able to make use of it in my finances. Besides, the purchasing power of the dollar was much higher at that time than today.

N: Yes, purchasing power is another issue. If the dollar has lost 90% of its purchasing power since then, you ought to repay 10 dollars today instead of only one.
But just think how much you would have had to toil for 275,000 dollars and place that in relation to what you could have earned with one dollar. There is no reasonable relation. The debtor has to render enormous services so that the lender receives their contractually agreed income - without doing anything in return.

WO: So you think we shouldn't get into debt?!

N: Debt isn't the problem. Or would you have a problem today with having to repay the one borrowed dollar – or, if you like, ten because the loss of purchasing power or fifty with a certain handling fee?

Everyone is silent.

N: Interest and compound interest is a rule of the game that is generally accepted and ensures the majority of people do most of their work not for themselves but for a minority of rich lenders, who, in turn, get richer and richer without doing anything. You could call that a modern form of feudalism.

I: So you would like to abolish interest?

N: Yes, I would.

WO: But then nobody would lend money anymore!

N: Not necessarily! For instance, there's no objection to a certain handling fee. Besides that, you can let your money work in another way. It is something concrete if, for example, you make an agreement to buy shares in a firm in return for a share in its profit.

WO: But that means profit without doing anything as well.

N: Not like in the interest system. For in this case you are participating in what is being generated with your money in the truest sense of the word. When there are losses, you have losses; when there is a profit, you make a profit. Then you get a stipulated share of the profit, which didn't, however, have to be made especially to pay the interest due to you.
       In the system of interest, on the other hand, a value has to be generated only because of the interest, even if the money just lies around and doesn't earn anything. Do you understand what I mean?

I: I think so. You mean that in a shareholding which leads to success all those who contributed to it have a share in the success, whereas in the system of interest the lender always gets their profit, regardless of what has happened to the money, even if it has been lost. In a shareholding the lender also participates in the risk or can increase their success if they otherwise contribute to the firm's success.

N: Exactly. That's what I mean by "concrete."

MO: Okay, I can understand that. All the same, I think you're exaggerating. Of course, the example you described to us is very impressive. But it shows an extreme case that has no meaning at all for everyday life. Nobody takes out a loan for 200 years. And most people only operate with borrowed money for a small part anyway.

N: But now I have to disagree with you. Basically we all operate with borrowed money. All money is issued by the central bank at some time – in return for interest. And so all of us – each individual and our entire economy – are affected by the interest rate screw. That is the actual reason why maximising profit has become the highest priority everywhere – even over dead bodies! And that's also the reason for the constantly growing tax burden. Now 80% of the tax we pay goes directly or indirectly to the banks. The public good doesn't benefit at all from this money but we all have to toil for it, getting more and more dependent on the big lenders and that's why our politicians do things that have less and less to do with the population's will.

i
p. 147

I: So you think that the ruthlessness in business life wouldn't be so great if the system of interest didn't exist?

N: There are doubtless always some greedy and ruthless individuals but at the moment every self-employed person is being downright forced to maximise their profit with all conceivable means in order not to go under.
Economies are made at the expense of quality and of materials and manufacturing methods that guarantee durability and long life; economies are made at the expense of nature, the environment and health; human misery in poor countries is consciously exploited and aggravated to further the price war in rich countries; public opinion is manipulated by advertising, politics by lobbying so that inferior and harmful products on grounds of ethics, morals, education and health can be offered and sold on a large scale; the media and even science are abused to withhold and distort the truth and artificially create unnecessary or even harmful needs and wants.
If at the end of the day more would remain over for everyone with less effort – if, for instance, the whole business here ...

He makes a sweeping gesture with his arms.

N: ... could be kept running with only 20% of our tax payments, what would that mean?

He pauses for a moment and looks around questioningly.

N: Don't you think that it would be better for everyone? Everyone would be more relaxed and have more time for themselves and their fellow humans. I think that chasing after money is a permanently fulfilling life task for only a few people.

I: You are certainly right about that.

There is a reflective silence.

MO: That's all well and good,

the man opposite interposes.

MO: But we still need growth. Our economy won't function without growth.

N: Because of the system of interest. Without interest there is no pressure to grow. Once a level we are all satisfied with has been reached, why does it necessarily have to go on growing?
It is the rules of the game in this financial system which not only force an unhealthy kind of economy on us but in actual fact a way of life in which the material aspect is unnaturally pushed into the centre.

I: And why doesn't anyone change that?

N: I don't think many people are really aware of this background. And those who pull the strings at the top are the ones who benefit from the system. They naturally do everything to ensure nothing changes – again almost like in the feudal system.

WO: But what's the goal of those people? They must be immensely rich!

N: Sure! All the same they want to increase their wealth – and above all their power – even more and of course keep their system stable. That's why they make sure this system appears to have no alternative and fight everything and everyone who takes action for people's freedom and independence.

That affects everything we have just spoken about: naturopathic medicine makes people more independent and more aware as well. So they fight it. Homeopathy puts the dominant position of the pharmaceutical industry at risk. So they fight it. On the other hand, not only can a great deal of money be made from vaccinations but they also make people dependent, sick and easy to manipulate in their fear of infection. So they are propagated.

MO: Now we've got back to the conspiracy theories. Those wicked boys obstruct everything that's good and further everything that's bad. That's really too stereotyped! And above all there is absolutely no possibility for change in your depiction, apart from violence, but then with real violence – revolution –, as here we have to do with people who have virtually unlimited means at their disposal.

N: Even if we disregard this conspiracy aspect – as you call it –, a change in our system is hardly conceivable anymore today. I agree with you on that. All the structures are already too ingrained and interlocked. All other areas are subordinated to the pressure for growth and profit that we've just talked about. The health service is mainly viewed from economic points of view, likewise the education system, and even nature conservation is subordinated to the economy.

WO: But the current health service is completely uneconomic. Huge sums are spent for procedures that aren't any help at all or at least are very ineffective. There would be many more inexpensive and more effective methods from naturopathic medicine or alternative medicine.

N: There you're right, of course. But that isn't considered at all. Rather, the focus is on a big economic sector – pharmaceutical companies, hospitals, nursing homes, etc – flourishing and doing well financially. After all, the paradox is that every sick person contributes to an increase in the gross national product through treatment, operations, medications, etc. – and that all the more, the sicker they are and the more costly and lengthy their treatment is.

WO: That's an awful view of things!

N: But it's the reality. If nobody was sick anymore from tomorrow, an enormous sector of the economy would be bankrupted, the stock market would plummet and our gross national product would decline. That would be a disaster from an economic point of view!
And so there isn't actually any real interest in a healthy population. In addition there is the fear of illness which makes everyone pay higher and higher amounts to the statutory medical insurance, take out supplementary insurances, and so on and so forth.

WO: I always say: Schools should actually teach how to handle the body properly to avoid illness. Basically that's part of general education.

N: But nobody is interested in that either. For the pupils are supposed to be educated to become well-qualified workers and unproblematic citizens. So you see the huge amount of subject matter which schoolchildren are already lumbered with today. You can't force yet another subject on them!

MO: If you take a close look, schools do exactly the opposite of helping children to have responsible, health-oriented lives. The insane pressure and stress that have become usual today make children sick – mentally and physically.

WO: And if they protest, they are sedated with drugs. Did you know that alone in the USA above 6 million children take Ritalin regularly?

☞ p. 182

N: And now we've got back to financial interests again.
But the entire situation is also completely stuck in a rut politically. To achieve a change in this educational system, unanimous decisions would have to be made in all federal states since they are responsible for education. So we don't need just one majority in the national parliament but 16 majorities in 16 state parliaments.

MO: There's no hope of that!

N: Yes, that's why I've given up hope that the system can be changed out of itself. Even if we had a selfless politician who can think clearly and doesn't just look beyond their nose to the next election, they still wouldn't be able to change much at first. First of all, they would have to be elected to an influential position, assert themselves there and then still find the necessary majorities to push through far-reaching changes in votes. In all this they would have to withstand party interests, competitors within their party, others parties and likewise lobby groups and powerful circles that steer public opinion via the media and finally – and now I unfortunately have to come back to the conspiracy aspect – they would have to be able to protect their life effectively. In the last few years some very clear-thinking politicians and hopeful people of influence have suddenly died in motor accidents or been found drowned in their baths or swimming pools! Do you really believe those were just chance strokes of fate?

Everyone is silent with shock.
The man opposite begins reflectively:

MO: What you say is interesting. I, too, have repeatedly thought about such incidents or other inconsistencies but in the end brushed it aside again. After all, I'm not a fan of conspiracy theories.

He smiles sourly.

MO: But I must say that the whole situation has increasingly come to a head in the last few years. Wherever you look, you actually only see dead-ends from which there seem to be no sensible ways out. For these very reasons I haven't voted for years. There aren't any real alternatives to choose from and besides that I also see non-voting as an expression of my protest. But of course it isn't a real solution. I wonder when we'll at last be offered a real solution as an alternative.

N: By who?

MO: Yes, by who ...!

sighs the man opposite fatalistically and stares into space with his eyes down.

I: Do you know?

I ask the man next to me.

N: Well, I do. Who, if not us? When, if not now?
I believe a lot of people think like you – and wait in lethargy. If all of them now awake from their lethargy, unite and become active, something new is bound to emerge, something better and future-oriented.

MO: You may be right but that requires a whole host of idealists to stand up and tackle things! But nothing like that is happening. Individuals are still too afraid to come out of their shells.

N: Luckily not all of them! There are very interesting developments concerning that. I'd like to read something to you briefly if you don't mind.

Everyone nods with interest.
He reaches into his briefcase and takes out a book. After leafing through it for a moment he finds the desired passage and starts to read:

N: *(1) The nation's health is a valuable asset and is under the special protection of this constitution. The state works towards its conservation and improvement in all fields.*

(2) The entire health care system is under the supervision of the state. There is only one national health fund. Surpluses generated are ploughed back into the state budget.

(3) The state shall endeavour to ensure that every citizen has the opportunity to maintain, restore or improve their health by themselves. Through its health and educational system it shall strive to make its citizens realise their own responsibility and work actively on their personal health. The state must help all Germans in this respect by providing appropriate education and information.

(4) Taxes can be imposed on products which impair or are likely to impair health.

He looks around at his listeners.

N: Well, how does that sound?

I: Interesting.

MO: Not bad. It sounds like something from the German Basic Law.

WO: The Basic Law? What are you talking about? The words "health" or "healthy" don't appear even once in the entire Basic Law! This is a completely different level. If that was law with us…!

N: I have a small addition from another article: *The state as an instrument of the citizens' will has the aim to provide every person with the greatest degree of happiness, self-determination, freedom, health, education and personal development.*

WO: Fascinating! By the way, the word "happiness" doesn't feature in the Basic Law either. I once researched that a while ago. But what was it you read aloud to us?

N: Those were extracts from Art. 19 and Art. 16 of the Constitution of the new German state, which was founded in 2012.

MO: I beg your pardon? New German state? Are you pulling our legs?

N: No, for goodness sake! Why should I do that?

MO: Well, I have never heard anything about it. Have you perhaps?

He looks around questioningly.
They all shake their heads.

I: No, not in the least! Something like that can't actually go unnoticed!

N: It obviously can, as you see!

MO: I guess that probably isn't regarded with approval by our establishment?!

N: Absolutely not. That's the reason for the silence in the mainstream media. But it exists. I have lived there with my family for five years.

I: How does the foundation of a new state work?

N: Founding a new state isn't difficult basically. But some requirements need to be met for it to have substance and make sense. In the general rules of international law a state is defined as a community which has a state territory, a state population and state authority.

i
p. 161

MO: ... and be recognised by other countries, or?

the man opposite interposes.

N: No, recognition isn't a necessary condition. Of course it is desirable in practice but it can happen at a later date. It's much more important for the state to have a structure and institutions that make it suitable for everyday life.

I: Does the new state have all that?

N: Yes, it has a constitution – which I have just read a few extracts from – it has a currency, a state bank, social security, an educational system. Some things still need to be organised – the state is still too small for that at the moment.

I: So what is the state called and where exactly is it located?

N: Königreich Deutschland (Kingdom of Germany).

MO: No ... Is that supposed to be a joke?

is the derogatory answer.

N: No, why?

MG: Kingdom! ... Somebody wants to make fun of us! Whoever wants another monarch with a sceptre and robe today!

N: Well, the British, Dutch, Belgians, Swedes, Danes, Norwegians and Spanish, for example. And do they make any impression of being backward? The sceptre and robe are incidentally only used for especially ceremonial occasions.

MO: But today we have a free democracy. Why should we decide on an autocrat?

N: As said, Great Britain, the Netherlands, Belgium, Sweden, Denmark, Norway and Spain are free democracies. There the monarchs are not autocrats. It's exactly the same in the Kingdom of Germany – and even more. Whereas kingship is handed down by inheritance from generation to generation in the other monarchies today, the Kingdom of Germany is an elective monarchy, meaning that the king is democratically elected. That is similar to the President of Germany, only that in this case the head of state is called "king."

But the difference is – and that's why the kings and queens are so popular in the other monarchies – that the king is completely outside the usual political scheming and becomes a superordinate focus figure who only changes every four or five years.

I: And who makes the laws?

N: Laws are passed by the State Council and the government business is conducted by the government. The king has nothing to do with that.

There is one thing that is new and unique in the Kingdom of Germany: Besides the legislative, judicative and executive powers there's a fourth power, the inspective. It consists of checking all laws, all administrative procedures, all government actions or a state organ or holder of office for conformity with the constitution and immediately revoking them if there is a violation. The king is the holder of this checking power.

I: So he is simultaneously something like the German Constitutional Court?

N: In principle, yes, or the Constitutional Court, which also exists in the Kingdom of Germany, is part of this inspective power. But the king also acts without anyone lodging a complaint. In Germany there have been countless violations of the Basic Law for many years. But nothing happens because nobody lodges a complaint. No matter if it is due to lack of interest or lack of money, the whole system gets more and more skewed. In the Kingdom that isn't possible as the king acts to ensure it as a guarantor of the constitution. If he detects a violation of the constitution, he can eliminate it immediately and even has the constitutional duty to restore the lawful state.

I: And is the king controlled as well?

N: Of course the king is also bound by the constitution. He can be removed from offices in case of a gross violation.

I: Oh yes! That's interesting.

MO: Yes, I think so, too,

  murmurs the man opposite me.

MO: How does the economy work? Rather capitalism or communism?

N: Neither or them. It is a new economic model that might best be described as "general welfare economy" According to the constitution, interest and compound interest are forbidden and taxes are only for steering purposes.

MO: What does that mean?

N: Direct taxes are voluntary as a rule. Taxes fulfil a positive purpose with us. For instance, they are imposed on products or activities which impair health or the environment so the damage isn't a burden on the population.

MO: And where is the government supposed to get money from?

N: The primary question shouldn't be where the government gets money from but how much money the government needs at all. This question appears in quite a different light in a society in which not everyone only thinks of themselves and not everyone wants to have everything from the government either. Just think how much money the government could save today if we weren't all so selfish – or didn't have to be to make ends meet. Then there would be much more room for everyone for charitable activities, etc. Then not everyone would have to turn to the government for help if they couldn't manage anymore.

MO: In other words, social benefits are transferred from the government to the citizens.

N: Look at it like this: people in a community are basically there for each other and anyone who has enough will scarcely turn away a begging hand. But in the usual social systems this charitable service is distributed and redistributed anonymously to everyone and so everyone pays for other people but for people they don't know and have nothing to do with. That's the price when the state as an institution is an intermediary between direct interpersonal relations. Then all humaneness is lost and because of bureaucracy, administration, etc. only a fraction of the total taxes reach those concerned.

I: And how does it work with you?

N: The individual municipalities do it in various ways. With us, for example, there is an office for mutual support. They have a long list of work to be done for the community or for other people who have registered minor or major projects with the office. At the same time it is recorded how many one-time or regular workers are required and how much will be paid for each project. In this way everyone always has possibilities of rendering services to others or the community and receiving something in return.

I: Is use made of it?

N: To an enormous extent! And by both sides! You wouldn't believe how many people work to keep the town, railway station, parks, etc. clean and are paid to do so, or engage themselves in helping in private households, gardens, etc. or projects they had never heard of before.
Now we don't have any more "social cases." Everyone gets a real chance to take the planning of their lives into their own hands and nobody has to feel like a supplicant or receiver of alms anymore as everyone does something and gets something in return.

I: That sounds very impressive.

WO: Yes, I think so, too.

MO: But the time will come when everything is nice and clean. And what happens when there are no new projects?

N: Now I believe that won't ever happen. The whole thing has developed such momentum as can scarcely be imagined. New contacts, groups, networks, new ideas, projects and concepts are being created constantly. It now goes far beyond repairs, clearing up, improvements, etc. with the establishment of entire business, artistic and craft ventures.

I: And where does people's motivation come from?

N: I think it's the normal natural motivation, human energy and drive that just needs to be freed from the yoke of an inhuman system.

MO: And if someone can't do anything because they are ill, for instance?

N: If they are ill, the health insurance fund takes care of it and there are always some people who don't register a project with the office for which they would like to pay someone but an amount to be donated to especially needy people. As already said, that is a very well-balanced system – and everything operates on the person-to-person level without any anonymous authority devoid of all humanity.

MO: All the same, your government will also need money.

N: Yes, of course, I didn't want to deny that. I just wanted to point out first of all that much less money has to be spent by the government when each person assumes more responsibility directly themselves.
The government obtains revenue through state-owned enterprises which also have to do with public good.

MO: State-owned enterprises ...

The man opposite me wrinkles his nose.

MO: For me that has the odour of communism, planned economy and state monopolies. All that didn't work in the past!

N: You're lumping several things together that don't belong together. Nobody has talked about planned economy or state monopolies. A sensibly managed, economically sound enterprise doesn't have to be bad only because it belongs to the state!
Particularly in the core sectors that have to do with the basic services for the population it's an absolute must to work with state-run industries. Anything else would be irresponsible. For otherwise meeting primary basic needs depends on a few private individuals striving for the maximisation of profit. Just think of the privatising of the water or electricity supply or the rail service! The results are strikes, train cancellations or delays because of technical problems, line closures, dismantling of tracks, often no

more service at stations because the station buildings have been auctioned off, fewer and fewer services and higher fares! The rail management doesn't care if the population is no longer satisfactorily served by them. The main thing is that the profit and the share price are in order. And the population doesn't have any possibility to influence things any more.

Then it is really better to have state enterprises as the management is subject to democratic control and the profits go to the government and therefore to the public.

MO: But everything stagnates without competition. There won't be any new, improved products when everything is run by the state.

N: No, it's not like that. You're again thinking of state monopolies that nobody wants. Anyone can start up their own private firm at any time and even the government can run several competing state-owned enterprises. But the basic services for the population lie in democratically elected hands and the government obtains revenues by doing something for the population and not just asking for money.

I: I find it a very interesting system.

N: And that isn't everything. The surplus from the health insurance fund also goes to the government. That means that the government has a fundamental interest in people being ill as little as possible, as it loses revenues with every treatment that is needed.

WO: Doesn't that result in the fund reimbursing only a little or reluctantly?

N: No, on the contrary almost everything is reimbursed. The principle is that anyone who heals is right. No strange restrictions exist that alternative practitioners are not allowed or that one medical remedy is permitted but another not, particularly if it is something natural or homeopathic.

Rather, people's own responsibility for their health is enhanced by seminars, training courses, information, etc. The government takes concrete action for people to live more healthily. I've got a few brochures with me. If you would like, you can have a look at them.

He gives everyone a small leaflet about "German Health," which is the name of the health insurance fund.

When he hands it to me, I ask immediately:

I: Could I also have a brief look at the constitution?

N: Of course.

He gives it to me.

It is a nice little bound book with a most ceremonial logo on the cover.

On the back I read:

With the foundation of the state "Kingdom of Germany" on 16.09.2012 the vision of a free state for all Germans became reality. The present constitution is the basis of a new future for all people. It shows how a state, as the instrument of the will of people, is solely the framework for happiness, welfare, meaningfulness and freedom. The Constitution of the Kingdom of Germany guarantees all these values. It is the order of creation cast in a legal form. Only such a system can have permanence and lead to lasting peace ...

Order of creation – what an unusual word in a modern document, let alone in a legal one! I have obviously come across an undertaking that is not just some ideological caper but something more far-reaching and of a profundity not so easy to grasp.

Lost in thought, I let my glance wander out of the window.

During this short train journey I have had so much food for thought and new impulses that it will probably take me a few weeks to digest all of them and classify them properly: The health problem, the immense dependence we have all let ourselves be manoeuvred into, although it would actually be reasonable to assume responsibility for ourselves, which is, however, always being made harder and reduced; then this insane pressure for growth and maximisation of profit on all levels, which ultimately cost us all more than it helps, with the health problem actually emerging as a symptom of the profit maximisation of the "health industry"; and the realisation that our interest-afflicted financial system is ultimately the root of the growth insanity and all the resulting problems. Only 20% of our taxes would be necessary for our common weal and the rest goes to the banks! Incredible! Why does everyone go along with it and doesn't change anything or at least protest? But actually the question has to be: Why do I go along with it, why don't I change something, why don't I go to the barricades? Out of ignorance? That is only part of the explanation. I could have opened my eyes and informed myself! Is it fear? Is it lethargy, as the man sitting next to me said?

It is admirable how much insight he shows into a lot of things and how nicely he conveys it, without superiority. I didn't even once have the feeling that he was pointing his finger even though he really "taught" us about a lot of things.

Yes, and on top of that the most astounding thing: the Kingdom of Germany, the existing solution to all these problems, in the middle of Germany, a state without taxes, without interest, with a completely new economic system. And I haven't ever heard anything about it! Actually I ought to have a look at it at once – and preferably participate in it. If a solution already exists and you don't have to search anymore, there is no reason to wait …

While my thoughts are flowing, the man sitting next to me turns to me:

N: Where are you travelling to?

I: Why do you ask?

is my perplexed reply.

N: Well, perhaps you might like to get to know the Kingdom personally? This train ends at the next station. Then you would only have to change once and would be there very quickly. I would be pleased to take you there … If you like!

I: That's very kind of you. Thank you very much,

I say, almost refusing, for after all I had planned my weekend quite differently. But hadn't I just realised that there wasn't any reason to wait any longer? So I spontaneously give myself a push and accept. If we are so close, I shouldn't let this unique opportunity go.

I give the constitution back to him, pack the leaflet and start to get ready to leave the train.

It all goes very easily and quickly, almost like flying, and we are already sitting in a smaller train which is to take us directly to the Kingdom.

N: By the way, my name's Norbert. As far as I'm concerned, we can use first names.

I: Yes, with pleasure. I'm Thomas.

It is already quite an intimate relationship, seeing that we only got to know each other such a short time ago.

I: How should I imagine it? Where are we going and what is awaiting me?

N: Well, nothing special actually. I don't want to tell you too much. You should be able to form your own opinion of it. We are now going to Talweis, a municipality in the Kingdom. There are now five municipalities in Germany. Talweis was the first one and it changed over to the Kingdom five years ago.

I: Changed over?

N: I'll explain that later. We have to get off in a moment.

I glance out of the window. We are approaching a small station. Actually it could be a typical small German station but I at once notice how well kept it is and how good the buildings look – rather untypical!
We take our suitcases and get off the train.
I look round attentively, expecting to see something spectacular, but I can't find anything striking. A reversed German flag with black at the bottom and gold at the top is fluttering above the station building.
I ask Norbert about it and he replies with a mischievous smile:

N: Another person who didn't pay attention at school?

I: What do you mean?

N: Well, I'm sure you've heard something about the Hambach Fest?

I vaguely remember opposition from the citizens, Vormärz, a big festival with demands for national unity, freedom and sovereignty of the people.

I: Yes, I have.

N: If you had looked closely at the pictures of the Hambach Fest, you would have seen the black-red-golden flag – from bottom to top.

I: Really? That was the original German flag?

N: Yes, it was: black to describe the night lying over Germany during its occupation by foreign powers, gold for the dawn of freedom gained and red for the great effort (translator's note: the German expression is "heart blood") with which it was won. Or at the bottom the earth on which people are striving towards the golden age with their life force. In the flag of the Federal Republic of Germany, on the other hand, the black is like a lid on everything else, burying life force and spirituality.
I look up at the flag again and notice that it not only consists of the three colours but also shows the crescent of a rising sun with beams. It is being illuminated by the late afternoon sun over the roof and makes a very promising impression on me.

We continue our way and leave the station.

N: If you don't mind, I suggest we walk a short distance. It's nice weather and it will certainly allow you to get a better first impression. Then I'll show you a small hotel where you can spend the night.

I: Okay, that's a good idea!

So we walk across the busy area in front of the station towards the pedestrian area.
It's crowded with people, many of them are shopping, others strolling around aimlessly, enjoying the pleasant sunshine. On the square and at the edges of the streets you can see some stands offering various goods, but also drinks and snacks.

I: Is it market day today?

N: No, why do you ask that? You mean because of the sales stands? It's almost always like that here. Since the changeover a lot of people have discovered this activity for themselves. That has led to a vitalisation of the pedestrian area. Most people enjoy the variety it provides. The streetscape is no longer so monotonous and uniform as it used to be. For instance, I often come here just to see what interesting things there are that day. And for the sellers it's a good opportunity to show their products and services, present their projects, establish contacts and of course earn money – all without a great fuss, investments or suchlike. All the complicated regulations there used to be have been done away with since the changeover and taxes, charges, etc. are also a thing of the past.

I: And that works? Without any rules or controls?

N: Yes and no. You know, we have introduced the so-called principle of trust. This assumes that everyone carries out their activities with full responsibility for themselves, their fellow citizens and their environment. That means everyone controls themselves and trusts that others do the same. That applies to all areas of life.

I: And that really works?

I ask again.

N: Yes, everybody makes sure their freedom stops exactly where it begins to restrict someone else's freedom. You wouldn't believe what an impact this principle of trust has had on most people. They no longer have the feeling of being observed, controlled and under surveillance everywhere and therefore being continually afraid of breaking some regulation or other. Instead we act in all conscience, with consideration of the environment and the people around us.

I: Oh yes. I can well understand that. I am just in the middle of a tax audit and know what control and surveillance feel like. The worst thing is that with this monstrous mass of laws and regulations there will always be an error to be found somewhere.

N: That is also certainly so intended. Insecure citizens, who always have a – potentially – bad conscience are easier to keep down without protests. In contrast, the focus with us is on human beings and their development, which is the reason for the principle of trust. Besides that, we have far fewer rules and they can be understood by everyone.

I: But that assumes a considerable development of consciousness in every person if everything is to function without any controls.

N: It's not really quite like that. Our Public Order Office in fact carries out sporadic controls as well, though only on a small scale and mostly incognito in everyday life. And serious offences which come to light or are reported by someone are also punished, according to type and severity. But above all, if someone is reported to have committed an offence, they become subject to regular, strict controls and nobody wants that. That alone is sufficient incentive to do everything correctly.

I: That virtually means you do things correctly not because you're controlled but so that you aren't controlled ...?

N: Yes, you could say it like that. At a first glance it looks as if there isn't any great difference. But psychologically or from a mentality point of view the difference is colossal.

We continue on our way. You can really observe a keen interest in the stands or vendor's trays.

I: Don't the shop owners mind so many competitors standing in the street here?

N: At the beginning they did. But now it has been shown that the shops' business is also stimulated by the larger number of people often walking along the streets. And some shop owners have joined in this trend by putting up a little stand somewhere farther away. Variety simply stimulates business while regimentation restricts it.

In the meantime we have reached the hotel, Hotel Rose. Norbert stops and shows me the entrance.

N: You can get a good and inexpensive room for the night here. And if you feel like it, there will be an interesting lecture followed by discussion on the history of Earth and the solar system in the Academy this evening. It starts at 7.30 pm right here, about 100 m in the cross street on the right. You'll see it straightaway as there will be a lot going on.

I: That sounds interesting. I'd be pleased to attend. Will you be there, too?

N: Yes, certainly. That's always a kind of highlight each month. I'll keep a seat for you. So see you there.

He shakes my hand cordially and vanishes into the crowd, waving to me again.

I take my suitcase and enter the hotel. It makes a very friendly impression on me – bright, fresh and clean. I go to the reception and ring the bell. The price list is hanging on the wall: 30 marks a night for a single room. Marks? Hm, how much might that be? I now realise that I don't know anything about the currency here.

"Good afternoon," I hear a friendly female voice say. I turn round swiftly in the direction it came from and see a brunette aged about 30 approaching me with an open smile.

W: You're looking for a room?

she asks.

I: Yes, but I've just realised that I have no idea what a mark actually is.

W: That's no problem. A lot of people who come here don't know,

she says with a smile.

W: The Reichsmark is the legal tender in our kingdom and at present it is worth about 13% more than the euro. That means 1 mark is equivalent to 1.13 euros.

I: Aha. Then you have really low rates. I'd like to have a look at a room.

My insecurity must be perceptible.

W: You're welcome to do so. But you don't need to have any doubts. When you come from outside, the price may seem very low to you. But don't forget that we don't have any taxes and the labour costs are lower as well, because there are simply far fewer deductions.
Come with me and I'll show you one of rooms straightaway.

She takes me up the stairs and along a short corridor to a room with a shower and toilet. It is really nice, bright and spacious with a view of a quiet courtyard. It is furnished with a wide bed, a bedside table, a table with two chairs, a TV set, internet connection, a wardrobe – nothing to complain about.

I: Really nice.

I say approvingly.

I: I'd like to take it.

W: Fine.

The woman laughs.

W: Then I'll give you the key. Breakfast is from 6.30 to 9.30 downstairs right next to the reception.

I: Do I have to sign up for breakfast and how much does it cost?

W: No, it's included in the price and you just come and help yourself from the breakfast buffet. How long would you like to stay?

I: Oh yes. Till Sunday.

W: Fine, I'll note that downstairs. So have a nice stay.

She departs and leaves me alone in the room.

Really incredible – such a nice room, including breakfast, for a little more than 34 euros, right in the centre of town! For that price I would have expected a musty room with old, creaking furniture, a sagging mattress and a mildewed bathroom.

Well, now I am in the Kingdom of Germany. What should I do next? At any rate I will go to that lecture in the evening. It sounds interesting, and the subject itself interests me as well. But until then …?

My stomach answers that question for me in a distinctly audible manner. I haven't eaten anything since the morning.

So off I go in search of something to eat in the Kingdom! I leave my things in the room and after a few steps am back in the busy street.

Before I can buy anything, I first of all have to change money. Therefore I first look for a bank. That should not actually be difficult in the middle of the pedestrian area but there are no bank signs in sight. Therefore I go to one of the stands and ask the seller.

S: A bank?

answers the man.

S: We haven't had any banks for a long time. They all had to go after the changeover.

I: Why was that?

S: We only have a state bank, the Royal Reichsbank. It's the guardian of our currency. That means that the entire economy can't be made to collapse for private profit anymore.
Do you want to change euros? If it isn't a large amount, you can do that with me, too. I can get rid of them again quickly.

I: Yes, I wanted to change 150 euros.

He hands me 150 Reichsmarks and adds:

S: If you give me 170, we can do it quite simply.

I: Okay.

I give him another 20 euros.

I: You don't seem to be so thrilled?!

S: Nobody here likes these notes. They also lose value rapidly and one day you won't get anything any more for them. I don't want that to happen to me. Our Reichsmark is something which has substance. It's genuine legal tender, not just a bit of paper.

I: What do you mean by that?

A: Well, for a euro note you only get something when someone else recognises it as a legal means of payment If nobody does that anymore, you have no legal claim to anything. Then you can smoke your note in your pipe, if you like.
With our legal tender you have a legal claim to a certain countervalue for every note. You can enforce your claim by legal action.

i
p. 157

I: Oh really?

A: Yes, that's why there's only one state bank. It makes sure that the money in circulation is always backed by the corresponding values.

I am dumbfounded. That is really a great difference to the euro, which has been printed in vast quantities for years without it being linked to any values.

I: Many thanks for the info – and for the money. Where can I get a bite to eat here?

A: Oh, just go towards the station and you'll find a lot of options.

I: Thank you very much. Good-bye.

As he had recommended, I go back to the station and look out for a snack bar or suchlike. But I cannot see any of the well-known signs and brands – no burgers or such things. At first I have difficulty in identifying the offers of food at all. It is noticeable how conditioned we are by trademarks and symbols. When you do not see the familiar signs, you have to look twice to recognise what is actually being offered.

But I finally find some snacks on offer. The most attractive thing my eye lights on is a small shop with a large window bearing a notice: *Delicious – Healthy*. Beneath I read on the shop windowpane:

> *Our principles:*
> *Delicious – for the eye and the palate*
> *Fresh   – ingredients and preparation*
> *Healthy   –*

and 3 crowns are stuck next to *Healthy*, one golden, one green, one blue and a green leaf as well.

A look inside the shop reveals a self-service counter with lots of small bowls and pots, fresh vegetables and fruit. Everything looks very appealing and I go inside.

At the counter you can put together a plate of salad from the various fresh ingredients, with a soup, a vegetable stew or rice with various additions. Everything looks very appetising and smells tempting.

I put together a large plate of salad and go to the cash desk. It is only 4 Reichsmarks. That seems too little to me. Therefore I ask:

I: Is that correct? It seems very little to me.

C: No, no, it's all correct,

answers the lady at the cash desk.

C: You saw that most of our ingredients come from the Kingdom.

I: No, I didn't see that.

C: The green crown there in the window.

I: Oh, I see. I was wondering what the crowns meant!

C: You probably aren't from here, are you? Then I'll be pleased to explain it to you.
You see, here in the Kingdom we have introduced some symbols which give information on the content, etc. at a glance. For instance, the green crown means that the ingredients or raw materials come from the Kingdom. In that way you know at once that the food was grown naturally.

I: Aha!?

C: Yes, other methods of cultivation are not allowed in the Kingdom.
The blue crown means that the raw materials were processed in accordance with the natural law directive and that nothing harmful or questionable was done there either.
And the golden crown finally shows that all the food ingredients are from the golden list at any rate. The golden list contains all natural and uncritical flavourings and stabilizers, etc. A food may only bear the golden crown when nothing else has been used.

I: That does sound complicated. Does everyone know what is in the list?

C: No, they don't. But in that way even those who don't know all the substances contained or don't have time to check out all the ingredients in detail can shop with awareness.

I: What isn't allowed in this list then?

C: For instance, most flavour enhancers, monosodium glutamate, artificial aromas, waste from slaughterhouses, which are usually so nicely called "mono- and diglycerides of fatty acids," chemically altered fatty acids, etc., that means everything most people don't give any thought to and which can lead to massive lifestyle diseases in the long term.

I: Does the green leaf also have a meaning?

C: Yes, of course. It shows that no animal substances have been used.

I: Okay. And if I'm looking for something vegetarian that may also contain dairy?

C: Well, the complete list of ingredients has to be stated on every product. Look here ...

She shows me a table hanging next to the counter.

C: ... you can find exactly what is in everything. We have especially mentioned what is <u>not</u> in it: meat, pork, eggs, cow's milk, and so on and so forth. In that way everyone can choose exactly what they want or what they want to avoid. The symbols are only supposed to be a rough orientation aid.

I let another customer who comes to the cash desk go past. When she has paid, I return to my original question.

I: And what do the symbols have to do with the price?

C: It's quite simple. When the ingredients come from the Kingdom, it has the side-effect that they are not taxed from the start and are therefore more favourable in price. Here all the fresh ingredients come from the Kingdom and we only buy rice and some additional products from outside. This means that almost everything is free of tax and charges from the beginning and you notice that in the price.

I am impressed. I had not thought of such chains of consequences at all.

I thank her, pay and sit down at a small table by the window so that I can watch what is happening in the street a little. There really is a lot going on outside but after all that is not surprising either, on such a splendid day in May. Hardly anyone can stay at home on such a day.

I enjoy my salad to the full. It is really very good and fresh. The tomatoes, the cucumbers – all very aromatic.

Just a moment – what about the tomatoes? I turn round abruptly to look for the cashier. She is standing just two tables away from me and clearing up.

I: Excuse me, how do you get tomatoes and cucumbers at this time of year if everything comes from the Kingdom?

She smiles.

C: Yes, that's fantastic, isn't it? One of our municipalities built huge greenhouses two years ago and established a state enterprise which grows all kinds of vegetables in them.

I: Then it has to be heated, doesn't it? That isn't very ecological!

C: Why not? They have a big zero-point energy generator to pro-
      vide heat and lighting for the greenhouses – simply with free en-
      ergy, without polluting the environment or wasting resources. I
      find that very ecological! They are even experimenting with trees
      now. Maybe we'll have home-grown avocados in a few years from
      now.

Free energy? I think I have forgotten to close my mouth again. At
any rate the lady looks at me in a very amused way. She comes over
to me and sits down at my table.

C: It's amazing what's possible when the basic rules of the game
      are changed, isn't it?

I nod. This new state is indeed getting more and more mysterious –
or better said, more fascinating. I have not even been here two hours
and have already seen and heard so many new things I never would
have dreamt of – and that in the middle of Germany!

I: How is all that controlled? I mean anyone can stick on some
      little crown and pretend.

C: Yes, you're right in principle. The crowns in the window are
      only indications. In reality we don't have the green crown for
      everything – only for the fresh ingredients. Therefore every dish
      on our menu is marked individually with all ingredients, as I
      showed you before.
      And controlling – we all control ourselves and each other. I don't
      know how to explain it to you. Somehow there has been quite
      a different atmosphere since the changeover. There's no funda-
      mental distrust as I remember there used to be, but trust. And that
      goes along with responsibility, care and charity. We really care
      about other people and want to do them good and not evil. It
      would never occur to me to want to cheat somebody. And it's like
      that with most people. Why should we want to cheat someone?
      What would it benefit us? You can see how favourable the prices
      already are. Why would we want to save another few pfennigs by
      tricking someone?
      There isn't such fierce competition as there used to be either.
      Somehow everything has become more relaxed. Even without

having to labour from morning till night you can make ends meet and have something over.

Here they want to reduce the regular working hours by one more hour so that there will only be a six-hour working day. We don't need longer to cover the costs of living. There aren't any taxes, almost everything has got cheaper, also because the burden of having to pay interest no longer exists.

I: Do you have a minimum wage?

C: No, that regulates itself automatically. Of course the town also helps. They have so much work to offer, for which they pay seven marks an hour. So of course every employer pays that as well, otherwise they would lose all their employees!

I: And does the town have so much money?

C: Yes, it does! Since the changeover our town has been doing brilliantly. No more debts, much less bureaucracy and adminis-tration, far lower energy costs, good revenues from the German Health insurance fund, the state enterprises are doing excellently and there is money from the Reichsbank for all value-generating projects. You can see what it looks like everywhere!

I: I haven't been here so long. Actually I've only just arrived – and can't stop being amazed at everything!

She laughs.

C: Yes, I've often seen that! And I bet you didn't know anything about us before.

I: Yes, that's true. Our media don't report anything about you!

C: No wonder! They're afraid that more town and villages will make the changeover.

I: Are there problems with the Federal Republic of Germany?

C: No, not any more. At the beginning it was quite different, espe-cially before we changed over. In the first Kingdom there were downright attacks and raids with a huge number of police. The German authorities broke their own laws on many levels just to harm the building up of the Kingdom. That was awful for the pi-

oneers at that time and a lot of them were demoralised.
However, I have to say that it motivated even more people. They were dissatisfied with the existing system and saw how the breaches and bending of the law by the German authorities were becoming more open and obvious. So there were demonstrations and finally our citizens compelled the holding of a referendum.

I: A referendum?

C: Yes, the inhabitants of Talweis pushed through their application for a referendum by collecting a large number of signatures.

I: What exactly does that mean?

I don't want to show so openly that I have never heard of such things.

C: Well, a referendum is, so to speak, a public vote on a particular issue. In order for such a referendum to be held at all, an application has to be made, supported by the signatures of a sufficient number of citizens.

I: And what was the vote to be conducted about?

C: About our town separating itself from the Federal Republic of Germany and joining the Kingdom of Germany.

I: What?

I exclaim in astonishment.

I: Is such a thing possible?

C: Yes,

the woman laughs back at me.

C: You can see it is. It worked with us.
Please don't ask me about the exact legal background, as I haven't really concerned myself with it. At any rate we decided in this way and then also implemented it legally so that our town freed itself from the Federal Republic of Germany.

p. 177

I: Well I never! Was everyone so sure that it was the right thing to do?

C: Not everyone, for sure. The outcome was not so overwhelming. About 55% voted for it.

I myself was mainly concerned about the school system. I was so frustrated because of my children. Two of them were already at school and were almost breaking under the insane pressure to perform, the chock-full curricula and the swamped teachers, and my third child was soon to start school. I had done virtually everything to find an alternative and I was even in a parent initiative which wanted to establish a new school with a different concept. But there was no chance. The laws and regulations were so rigid that the best possible thing was to establish a new school, which, however, had to function according to the same principles as all the existing ones.

I nod. I can very well understand what she is talking about. Our school system is so outdated and ineffective that it long ago ceased to meet the requirements of our time and people. It emerged from the ideas of the industrial revolution, where everything revolved around fixed norms, quantitative specifications, measurable efficiency, machines which can be dismantled into or assembled from individual parts, etc. That is why the children are divided into classes according to age, taught in strictly defined lessons in accordance with specified collections of teaching material – and that after a quasi-military model, where they have to reproduce specific memorised answers and preferably get out of the habit of questioning things themselves.

I: And the Kingdom provided better alternatives?

C: Yes, of course. Its constitution says that school should make people into self-confident, holistically developed personalities and that the curricula have to be holistically oriented towards life. Here the state doesn't obstruct but promotes the establishment of new schools – also with alternative concepts.

That's why our parent initiative only saw one possibility of implementing our plans. We had to leave the prevailing legal system and system of government. Nothing else really interested me so much. Of course economic, social and environmental aspects were also big issues at that time. But as I said, I was concerned about the school system and my children.

I: And have your hopes been fulfilled?

C: Oh yes, more than that! Immediately after the changeover we were able to set up a new school, even though we wanted to implement an unusual, absolutely revolutionary concept, the Shetinin concept. I don't know if you've heard of it.

She looks at me questioningly.

I: No, it really doesn't mean anything to me.

C: It's a school concept that was developed in Russia. In principle there aren't any lessons as we know them. The children teach each other with their own rhythm and complete the entire subject matter of the Abitur (German university entrance qualification) in two to four years.

I: I beg your pardon? In two to four years? How does that work?

C: Yes, my older son did his Abitur at 15. My second one was even faster because the system was already established.

I: That's incredible. I just can't imagine it.

C: Yes, I can understand that. You have to look more intensively – and also practically – into it before you can see how that's possible.

I: Isn't that an even greater time pressure for children than in a traditional school?

C: No, there isn't any time pressure anymore. There are no requirements. The children are finished when they have grasped the knowledge and successfully implemented it. That sets the framework – individually for each child.

I: And what do the children do when they finish school so early?

C: My older son did a craft apprenticeship and is now studying. My second son is still going to school. There are now schools of further education, which teach things nobody used to have time for.

I: What, for example?

C: Well, higher natural sciences, knowledge and skills regarding body and mind, etc. All possible things that build on and deepen the old Abitur knowledge.

I am speechless. I had not expected anything like this. I cannot classify any of it in my mind. I cannot even imagine it, so that I cannot ask any more questions about it.

Somehow the lady must have read all that from my face. At any rate she looks at me as if she has.

So as not to appear quite so stupid, I therefore murmur:

I: Very interesting, really very interesting!

and follow up on my previous question:

I: Then it has really been worthwhile for you!

C: Absolutely! And not only with regard to the school. So many things that I would earlier never have dreamt of have altered since the changeover.

You know, it is of course somehow clear that it is economically good when there aren't any taxes or interest any more. But you don't actually think it will go into your very own personal life feeling.

I: What do you mean?

C: Well, in the years since the changeover the burden of expenditure has decreased so much for each of us that we need to spend much less time on earning our living. As I said, the weekly working hours have already been cut in most sectors. Suddenly you can occupy yourself with other things that are actually much more interesting and more important for life but there used to be hardly any time for in the rat race.

In the meantime, earning a living is no longer the most important part of life and other things already occupy at least an equally important place for many people.

I: What, for instance?

C: Family, art and music, the public good. Just look around our town. There aren't any dirty places or eyesores anymore. In the towns there are initiatives by residents who together keep their neighbourhood in order and beautify it. Just like that, voluntarily, on an honorary basis, without money, without being asked to, without stress. That is great fun, brings everyone closer together and fills us with pride, when we walk through the town and are just happy at how lovely and clean everything is. I never used to have such a feeling. But then the stress never allowed me any time to think about such things.

She glances at her watch.

C: Oh, I've been chattering at you for ages,

she says in alarm.

C: That wasn't actually my intention,

she adds almost apologetically.

I: No, no, it was very interesting. I have got a lot of food for thought. Thank you very much.

C: I'm glad about that. Now I have to clear up a bit in the kitchen. Enjoy your meal.

With these words she stands up and busily hurries off.

I remain sitting quite a while feeling numbed. I have even completely forgotten my meal. What I have learnt in that brief conversation is more incredible and shocking than the fact that there is a new state in Germany, which is a kingdom with its own currency. For it is not a question of outward and organisational things but of really fundamental aspects of life: a stress-free community with less and less pressure to work for the material necessities of life and more and more time for oneself and the public good, in addition a school system without pressure, in which the children do their Abitur in a few years and can then get into far deeper fields.

Those are things that cannot just be changed by pressing a button. A new currency is quickly made but up to now I have scarcely thought it possible anymore to remove fear, pressure and competitiveness from people's consciousness. And that has happened here! In just five years! And without revolutionary changes! The town does not look fundamentally different from other towns in Germany, neither do the people. Only a closer look reveals the differences or when you speak to people. But I have got an idea of what you would find if you could look into people's hearts.

And it cannot even be imagined what further developments there will be in the coming years. It is fantastic, outrageous and even more revolutionary than if all the buildings were turned upside down.

Outside a child walks past and waves to me through the window. It smiles and its mother, following its gaze, also smiles at me. I smile back. Aren't the people here in general more friendly and relaxed? I look on to the street in all directions and think back to my hotel and further back to the station, when I got off the train. I don't remember a single face that did not somehow radiate harmony and joy ...

But that was nonsense, just lyrical idealisation! I cannot remember it all exactly and it might also just be chance. Everyone is in a better mood on such a nice sunny May afternoon ...

I make myself return to reality, see that I have not finished eating my salad and hurry to do so. I ought not to idealise but rather be more critical. I still know much too little about the whole thing and have only spoken to a few people. But in the meantime I have endless questions. Let's see how I will get them all answered.

When I have finished, I stand up, put my plate on the shelf for used crockery and leave the restaurant. The cashier is no longer to be seen.

Outside I step into the sun, which is standing low on the horizon. It dazzles me and bathes everything in its orange-red rays. The street is still busy. I stroll past the stands and shops, looking at what they offer. I do not notice any really spectacular differences.

Then I come to a shop with newspapers and books. That now interests me very much and so I go inside. In the big display on the wall I see the well-known papers and magazines but also some others I have never seen. Their headlines surprise me as they differ greatly from those of other newspapers. I am used to just having to look at two or three papers to know what is in all of them. The reporting in the media has been increasingly standardised for years. Somehow they all seem to get their information from the same source and also take it over word for word so that the articles or TV and radio reports are almost identical.

But here I find completely different reports, some of them on different topics, some of them also with conflicting opinions. One paper especially strikes my eye: *Die schöne Welt* (The Beautiful World) with the subtitle *Good News of the Day*. In it there is in fact only positive news, and by no means only banal topics. Everything is to be found – business, politics, health, German news, international topics – but always with a positive slant. An interesting approach that I have not seen before.

I want to have a closer look at all that, so I buy a whole pile of newspapers to study later in peace. On the way to the cash desk my glance falls on a strange paper. It has a "?" as title. I pick it up and leaf through it a bit. Its credo is "Courage to question". It is opposed to the accepted custom of journalists only to present finished, complete answers, even if these are by no means certain. The main article is about the Ukraine and presents the various viewpoints and opinions very controversially without preferring one or other of them from the start. After skimming through the articles, I cannot at least say which opinion the author favours, which I find interesting. Balance and critical journalism have become rarities in the last few years. So I put the paper on my pile as well and go to the cash desk. I notice that the papers I buy are almost all about 25% cheaper than the comparable ones I know. I wonder whether the price is supposed to determine the customers' selection.

I ask the man at the cash desk about the price difference but he just replies laconically:

MC: Well, it's clear! Nearly all of them come from the Kingdom – tax-free and on paper from the state forests.

I: So it isn't an attempt to get people to read a particular preferred representation?

MC: Yes, of course, the truth! That's the constitutional duty of the press.

I: And who controls that?

MC: Everybody. Also the press itself. Haven't you read the daily paper today? I see, you aren't from here. Have a look at this.

With these words he pulls an already well-read newspaper from under his table. The front page is emblazoned with a correction in large letters. I am dumbfounded.

MC: Someone strongly attacked the mayoress in the town council meeting last week because of some business transactions. That's neither here nor there. At any rate the man was torn to shreds by this newspaper the following day. They reported lots of things he'd done ... His credibility was completely destroyed. Well, he has now obviously been able to prove that nothing of it was true – confusions, wrong interpretations, gossip. That's why the newspaper is printing a detailed correction today – in the same size and format as the original article – just as the constitution lays down. And don't you believe that the mayoress is particularly glad about it. Now she has to seriously face up to these reproaches!

I: Does something like that often happen?

MC: Well, what is often? Normally the newspapers make sure that everything is correct. Such corrections appear from time to time. That always makes the matter very interesting.

He smiles.

I thank him and leave the shop. I'm again seized by a tingling feeling. That can scarcely be true. For years I have been annoyed about the almost completely standardised press, where you have to search the internet laboriously to see any different opinion whatsoever, and here – in the middle of Germany – true, honest journalism par excellence is being practised … Incredible!

There are not so many people in the street anymore. Dusk is slowly starting to come. I look at my watch and realise that it is not long until the lecture and my appointment with Norbert.

Where was it again? Oh yes, in the other direction. Then I will pass my hotel again on the way. So I can leave the pile of papers in my room and at the same time put on a jacket. It is starting to get a bit chilly.

I hurry to my hotel and then continue, as Norbert described to me. When I turn into the street he mentioned, I see a considerable crowd heading for the entrance of a historic building. It may be from the Wilhelminian time, and a plaque near the entrance says: *Royal Academy for Knowledge, Wisdom and Self-Development.*

I go inside, pay the entrance charge and then follow the other people to the lecture hall on the first floor, which is actually nearly full.

Now I have to find Norbert. He wants to keep a seat for me but he did not say where. I scan the rows with my eyes but cannot see him. Maybe he is not there at all? However it may be, I now have to find a seat as long there are some still free. I slowly push through a row and go downstairs. There I suddenly see Norbert – at the speaker's lectern! Well I never! Is he perhaps the lecturer? I go right downstairs and approach. He sees me and comes over to me.

N: Hallo, there you are! I thought you'd had second thoughts about coming.

I: No way! But if I'd known you were giving the lecture.

N: No, no,

Norbert says dismissively.

N: I'm only doing the introduction. But now you must quickly find a seat. It's going to start in a moment. Do you see the two empty seats over there? Next to the gentleman with the moustache and the young man with the long, fair hair. You can sit there and I'll come in a few minutes.

I quickly find the seats – in the front row, of course! I explain to the gentleman and the young man that one of the seats is reserved for me.
The man shakes my hand and the young man says:

YM: Yes, yes, I know. Norbert told me about it. Good evening, I'm Joachim.

I: I'm Thomas.

I quickly sit down, interested to see what will happen next.
After a few minutes a booming gong sounds. Then Norbert goes up to the microphone and holds a brief opening speech in his capacity of Director of the Academy! Wow, so that's who he is!
As he says, such a lecture by a guest scientist – today Monsieur T. from France with simultaneous interpretation – takes place regularly once a month. The subject is *Was the history of Earth and our solar system quite different from what we thought?*
The gentleman next to me and Joachim stand up and go to the front, where they take Norbert's place at the lectern.
Then the lecture starts. So the gentleman with the moustache is Monsieur T., a geologist from Paris. He might be in his late forties. Joachim translates his lecture into German, which he does excellently, although I guess that he is not even 18.
The main thesis of the lecture is that Earth did not develop through tiny little changes over infinite periods of time into its present state but that there were a series of cataclysmic interactions with other bodies in the solar system, which caused the geological changes within a very brief time. These were impacts of meteorites, near-collisions or near-encounters with other planets or electric discharges between the

planets. These processes shaped Earth's surface, created mountains, shifted the continents and even tilted Earth's axis.

He explains all this very graphically and intelligibly with good visuals – a successful, diverting lecture.

Then comes the second part of the evening – the discussion. Here anybody can ask questions or join in the discussion. Norbert goes to the front again to moderate this part of the evening.

There are a lot of questions and contributions of very different kinds – scientific and banal, questions of comprehension and counter-arguments. I am really surprised how actively the audience participate. But I am most surprised by Joachim's linguistic skills, which are now really tested as he has to translate continually back and forth in the two languages.

After a while a boy of about 13 or 14 speaks.

B: You mentioned that the last extra-terrestrial event that was important for Earth's geology was a meteorite strike, which happened about 10,000 years ago. Where do you get this figure from?

T: From ice cores.

B: Can you please explain that in more detail?

T: That isn't actually the subject of this evening.

Now Norbert intervenes.

N: Excuse me, Monsieur T. I explained the basic principle of our Academy to you beforehand. The basis of every single finding, statement, theory or piece of knowledge is examined and, in turn, the foundation of this basis until we arrive at basic facts or assumptions that we do not have to substantiate further. Only when this chain has been completely examined and verified do we view the statement or finding as valid. That's why it is important for us here to answer such questions about the basis conscientiously.

Joachim translates and Monsieur T. then continues:

T: Yes, excuse me, I had forgotten. That is otherwise not customary, which is why I am not used to it.
     So for an ice core you drill a hole in the ice sheet on, for instance, Greenland or the Antarctic and examine the ice core obtained.

As you know how much snow falls annually and how pressure compresses this amount of snow into ice, you only need to measure how deep a particular event lies and can then convert it into years.

B: Is it correct that it is a requirement that the same amount of snow falls each year?

T: It doesn't have to be exactly the same amount but an approximate uniformity is a requirement.

B: How does the amount of precipitation change after a large meteor strike?

T: That depends on many single factors. But with large meteor strikes, especially when they strike the sea, the precipitation is estimated to be from 5 to 10 m of rain a day for several weeks.

B: That means 50 to 100 m of snow a day in the cold regions?

T: Yes, that may be correct.

B: But then the ice cores are valueless. If as much snow falls on one day as otherwise in a whole year, you don't have the possibility of dating the meteor strike anymore.

Monsieur T. looks at the boy without speaking.
At last he seems to reflect again and says with a strange smile:

T: Now I know why some of my colleagues warned me about the Academy. I really can't answer that question. I myself don't make any ice core analyses. I will have to speak to a colleague who is specialised in that and ask if they somehow consider those things. But to be honest, I very much doubt it. It can well be that all the events I talked about took place much nearer to the present time.

The boy thanks him and sits down again.
The discussion goes on for almost another hour. The whole thing is well done, diverting and varied. Monsieur T. sometimes really does not have an easy time. People ask questions which are outside his field of specialisation. Thus a woman asks:

LA: Disasters are often judged from a moral or karmic viewpoint, meaning they represent expiation or punishment for offences.

Have you ever examined the disasters you have investigated and particularly their chronological classification in that respect?

T: That assessment is only relevant for events that happen in connection with human beings. For all incidents at a time when no humans or human culture yet existed, this question has no importance.

At this point the boy who had asked the question before raises his hand and is immediately called upon to speak by Norbert.

B: But with an altered chronological classification that might look quite different. Humans may already have existed when the continents separated or the mountains were created.

T: Yes, that can't be refuted. As I already said before, I haven't made any investigations in that direction so far.

Another question comes from an elderly gentleman:

G: If other planets have engendered geological changes on the earth, then, in turn, we should also be able to find traces on these planets.

T: Yes, that's a very interesting point, which we have only recently begun to research. The first indications show that the extreme surface structures on Mars were generated by electric discharges between the planets.
Earth's moon was likely also affected by near-encounters with other planets. It was probably at least once so greatly heated that its surface liquefied and bubbled. The remains of these bubbles are the great seas which were up to now believed to be craters but actually do not display the typical features of craters.
But that's a different topic, which would provide material for a whole evening.

Finally Norbert closes the question time, thanks all those present and the participants, announces the next lecture in four weeks and brings the evening to an end.
There follows a long burst of applause and then the meeting ends.
I stand up and go down to the three. Norbert congratulates Monsieur T. and Joachim. When he sees me, he turns to me and says:

N: Ah, Thomas. We are going for a drink. Do you want to join us?

I: Yes, I'd love to.

I join them and together we slowly make our way out together. Norbert takes us purposefully to a small pub nearby, where we sit down at a table in the corner and order something to drink.

I: Congratulations,

I start the conversation.

I: That was really a successful evening – and very well attended for a scientific lecture!

N: That's nothing unusual. These evenings have enjoyed great popularity from the beginning. You could see that from the lively discussion.

I: Do you always invite particular people?

N: Actually that's a part of the Academy programme and how it all started. In the Academy we invite a specialist to visit us for a week every month. They are available to our pupils and students to clarify special questions that have arisen in processing their knowledge or creating syllabuses.
      Besides that, they hold a public lecture for the general population, like this evening. Then he holds a specialised lecture in the Academy, also followed by a discussion, and finally he attends a meeting of our "pioneers." That is a small closed group that is concerned with special subject matter, with no admission to outsiders.

I: A kind of secret society?

N: Yes, you could say so. We have simply realised that not all knowledge or research is suitable for the public. Many things risk not being understood, misunderstood, falsely interpreted or wrongly applied. Then it's better to keep them initially within a small circle of people with like-minded thinking and similar awareness.

I turn to Monsieur T.

I: So you have even more up your sleeve than what you told us this evening?

Joachim translates.

T: Yes, of course. The public can't understand a lot of things at all. And every scientist also has thoughts and reflections they would never speak about in public but which they would be glad to talk about with colleagues.

Then I ask Joachim:

I: And how do you actually know French so well. That was really perfect. Are you French?

YM: No, but I went to school in France for about two years.

N: Joachim did his Abitur at the age of 14 and then went to France. We have some pupils who use their early Abitur to perfect a foreign language abroad afterwards. They have completed their schooling but still go to school only because of the language and the contacts.

I: I'm really impressed. I was equally impressed by the young man who asked the question about ice cores.

N: Yes, he started studying at the Academy straight after his Abitur. He has now completed his basic studies and wants to specialise in geology and palaeontology.

I: But he isn't older than 15, is he?

N: Yes, that's right, he's 14.

I: How long do the basic studies last then?

N: Two years.

I: Then he did his Abitur at 12? He was a child prodigy, wasn't he?

N: That isn't as uncommon as it appears when you come from outside. With us you can theoretically master the entire Abitur knowledge in one year. But that's the exception. But two to four years are completely normal.

I: And how do you do that?

N: I can't explain that in a few words. Ultimately, you have to experience it for yourself. For if you have gone through the classic school system you will be marked by it.

The crucial thing is that the children acquire the knowledge playfully themselves or teach it to each other. They organise their day themselves, continually rework the entire curriculum themselves and prepare the knowledge for the following generation.

That all happens in such a joyful and motivating way that the children suck up everything like a sponge, just as they can retell an exciting good-night story to you weeks later.

I: Did you go to school in this system?

I ask Joachim.

I: How did you perceive the difference …? But you can't compare it with the old system at all.

YM: Actually, I can. I went to school in France for two years and there they have the traditional system.

I: And how was that for you?

YM: Funny. I mean, I basically already knew everything. But I have often wondered how the others understand it or they often didn't understand it, which is no wonder for me. Those boring, often disconnected upfront lessons and the continual interruptions! You have scarcely immersed yourself in a topic when the lesson is at an end and you begin with a new subject. There's no better way to create confusion!

I: Oh, so it isn't like that here?

YM: No! You only study one subject until you've finished it and then begin the next one.

I: What do you mean "until you've finished it"?

YM: We begin each subject at its origin and then deal with the subject matter up to the Abitur. When we have finished, we begin with the next subject and then each subject in turn according to how they build on one another.

I: And if you don't understand something?

YM: We don't just get it presented to us like in the old system. We get it presented in our groups and then work on it independently for ourselves.
Besides that, the cycles are always repeated. If you've got stuck somewhere the first time, you can take it up again the second time round. In this way everyone understands it sooner or later.

I: I see! That's how it happens that one person is finished at the age of 12 and another not until 14?

YM: Exactly.

I: And how are you examined?

YM: Not at all. We don't have any exams or marks. Since everyone is not only a pupil but also a teacher for the younger ones, it becomes obvious every day where you have gaps. And all the gaps will be filled at the latest when you are sitting on the curriculum commission.

I: And whatever do the teachers do then?

I turn to Norbert.

N: The teachers are the pupils themselves. The adults are only learning mentors who are available when there are questions or supervise the whole process so that everything runs smoothly.
Oh, who's there?

he suddenly calls loudly in the direction of the entrance.
A tall, stocky man in his mid-thirties, who has just come in, turns to us and approaches us with a broad grin.

N: Hallo Dieter! Long time, no see!

D: Hallo Norbert. Hallo everyone,

he adds for our benefit.

D: Well, it was your great evening again today. Unfortunately I couldn't come. Was it good?

We all nod simultaneously.

N: Yes, it was super. You really missed something.

But come and take a seat. Or have you got an appointment?

D: In a certain respect but I have half an hour before that.

N: May I introduce you. Our guest lecturer, Monsieur T. from France. You know Joachim and this is Thomas. He's looking round the Kingdom for a few days.

D: Very pleased to meet you.

He sits down, orders something to drink and then turns directly to me.

D: How long have you been here?

T: I only arrived today.

D: Well, that isn't very long. So you probably haven't seen much.

T: Quite a lot. But I first have to digest what I've seen and heard. I already don't know if I'm awake or dreaming.

I say with a laugh

D: Yes,

he laughs in his turn.

D: I believe that. I haven't been here so long either and I felt exactly the same at the beginning.

T: Aha! How long have you been here?

D: I finally moved here two years ago. Then I set up my firm.

T: What do you do, if I may ask?

D: I'm a carpenter and have a workshop for furniture and interior fitting.

T: Interesting. And you're doing well?

D: Very well. I'm very satisfied.
    And you? What are you most interested in?

T: Everything actually. I didn't know until today that the Kingdom existed at all.

D: And you came here straightaway? I call that being consistent.

T: Yes, Norbert invited me and so now I'm here!

D: With Norbert you have the best guide. He can explain everything to you better than anyone else!

N: Now, now,

Norbert interposes.

N: But tell me, will you be there tomorrow?

D: At the town council meeting? Of course. Won't you be there?

N: Yes. I will. I only meant because you weren't there last time.

D: Yes, I was travelling. Well, how's Sabine?

N: Fine, she's very well.

D: I'm glad to hear that. But I think I have to go. I was glad to meet you. Have a nice evening.

He shakes everyone's hands.
When it's my turn, he says:

D: If you're interested, you could visit my firm some time.

I: I'd love to but I'm leaving on Sunday.

D: Think about it. Norbert can tell you where we are. So good-bye!

He raises his hand in greeting and leaves.

N: Yes, that would be really interesting. It's a wonderful business, straight out of a picture book.
But now I have to go as well. My wife is waiting for me. Would you like to come over to our place for coffee on Sunday?

I: I'd love to. But something else that would interest me is the town council meeting you talked about. Is it open to the public?

N: Of course, the constitution prescribes that. It's tomorrow at 3 pm in the town hall, really easy to find.

With these words he gets up.

N: I wish you a nice evening. The drinks are on me.

He takes his leave and goes to pay.

We three remaining ones stand up as well. I'm starting to feel tired. No wonder with the mass of impressions I've had today. I say good-bye to the others and leave the pub.

Outside it is dark and peaceful. I enjoy the fresh air and slowly go back to my hotel. In my room it is so quiet that I can actually hear my thoughts flying. When I want to lie down in bed after my evening routine I discover a card on my pillow saying "Spelt – only the best for your head!" Below follow brief instructions on how to handle it best.

I stretch out comfortably, bed my head as recommended and at once notice how my whole spine is being pleasantly extended. The mattress is certainly also something special. But after this day all that does not astonish me anymore.

For a while I review everything I have seen and experienced today and then fall asleep.

When I wake up again, it has already got light. I feel more refreshed and well-rested than I have for a long time. I quickly jump under the shower and then go down to breakfast. The other guests have prob-ably all left or I am the only one. At any rate I can help myself to the buffet alone.

Today I want to explore the town more thoroughly, a bit away from the centre as well. So I set off and march as the whim takes me along big and small streets, side streets, footpaths, through shopping areas, residential areas and allotments. The weather is nice and it does me good to be in the fresh air.

Regarding the appearance of the buildings, the town does not make an essentially different impression on me from any other small Ger-man town. The only not so usual thing is a simple, but striking build-ing at the edge of the town centre. It is obviously a new building but it combines older styles of architecture. I cannot really classify the whole thing. When I get nearer, I see on a sign that it is a synagogue. Everything is quiet and nobody is to be seen. But the large numbers of cars in the car park indicate that the Sabbath day church service is probably taking place.

But the streetscape is a bit different in a subtle way. After I have passed through several streets, I become aware, for instance, that I have not seen any banks and only one pharmacy. That is already re-markable for they are usually part of the normal street scene. In other towns there are so many pharmacies that I have often wondered if they really all have sufficient business. Is that chance here? Or are there really fewer pharmacies in the Kingdom? There is yet another question to which I should look for an answer.

With regard to the banks, I have already learnt that there is actually only the Royal Reichsbank.

I also see relatively little product advertising. When there are plac-ards somewhere, they mainly advertise events. Instead, sales or infor-mation stands are to be found in many places, as I saw yesterday.

When I am a bit farther from the centre in an area with detached houses, I suddenly hear noises like on a building site – a circular saw, hammering, electric drills and loud shouts. I go round a corner and see a plot with about 15 people who are obviously busy erecting a large wooden garden house and a wooden fence. On the pavement is a pile of boards, which are to be gradually cut to size and used for the construction.

I go nearer and have been watching the work for quite a while, when an elderly woman approaches me and addresses me:

EW: Hallo, have you also registered for today?

I: Registered?

I ask perplexed.

I: No, I haven't.

EW: All right. I only thought so because you were standing around as if you had been invited and not collected. But everyone is there according to my list.

I: Sorry, I don't know what it's about. I have just been admiring the zealous workers here. If you keep on like that, you'll be fin-ished in a few hours!

EW: Yes, That's how it's planned. At the beginning we registered the project with the office with a duration of three to four weeks. But then we got so many job applications that we thought we'd let them all come and complete it in one day.

I: Is that the Office for Mutual Support?

EW: Yes, and then a few people contacted us privately as well.

I: And what do the neighbours say about the noise today?

EW: They are part of the project. My husband helped one of them put up wallpaper last year and I babysit the others' small children now and then. You scratch my back and I'll scratch yours. We've been doing that for years.

I: Super. I wish you every success with the project.

EW: Thank you and have a nice day.

I go on my way.

When I reach the outskirts of the town with the first fields and meadows after a while, I see at some distance quite a lot of people working in a field. When I get closer, I see that they are spreading straw. It is a motley crowd of people – young and old, men and women and also children. At the edge of the field lies a large pile of straw bales, and a folding table with drinks and snacks is standing next to it with a bench, on which some people are sitting and resting. A good atmosphere seems to prevail; at any rate I hear frequent laughter, jokey exclamations and suchlike.

I go closer to find out what exactly they are doing. When I get to the table, an elderly man is just coming from the field.

I: Hallo, may I ask what you are all doing here?

EM: Hallo. Of course you may. But first of all I must have a little drink.

He gets himself a glass of water and then turns to me again.

EM: Well, young man, you probably aren't from here.

I: No I'm not. I'm just here for the weekend and am having a look round.

EM: Oh yes. That's good! Carry on! We're mulching our potatoes here today.

I: Oh I see.

EM: We planted them a month ago and now that the foliage is starting to grow we're mulching them with straw.

He probably sees from my face that this statement does not mean much to me and goes on.

EM: Mulching is better than earthing them up. The layer of straw not only prevents the potatoes growing up into the light and getting green. It also prevents weeds, loosens the soil and keeps it moist, even in summer.

I: Aha, I understand. And who are you doing the work for?

EM: Who for? Well, for us.

I: But there are a lot of people working here.

EM: Yes, a nice thing, isn't it? They're all working for themselves and for the others at the same time.

I: And who does the field belong to?

EM: The town. Our association enquired about unused land and they made this field available to us.

I: And how do things go on after that?

EM: Well, when the plants are bigger, we'll come regularly and collect potato bugs and otherwise make sure that everything is all right. Everyone works four hours a week. And then we harvest the potatoes in the autumn.

I: And what happens to the crop?

EM: Everyone takes what they need. Part of the crop is of course kept for planting next year.

I: That's interesting!

EM: Yes, it is, isn't it? It's a brilliant idea. For an absurd four hours a week you can get the best, untreated food – like from your own garden but with much less work.

I: And it seems that a lot of people participate!

EM: Oh yes! There are more and more each year. The town has also increased the area every year. Over there, for example …

He points to the neighbouring field.

EM: ... we sowed sweet corn there last week.

I: Sweet corn!?

EM: Yes, that's a rewarding food in summer, ideal for barbecues and much more healthy than meat.

I: Isn't that a lot of effort for a few corncobs?

EM: No, you're mistaken. You actually only have to hoe well at the beginning so that the weeds don't get out of control. That's peanuts with so many people. And that's very communicative work, when you go through the rows next to each other with your hoes. And we expose the seeds before sowing them. Then they have a fivefold yield.

I: I beg your pardon? You expose them?

EM: Yes, don't you know that? It's brilliant. The seeds are placed in an electric tension field for a few days before sowing. That restores the genes to their original state. Then the seeds germinate better, are much more resistant to pests and have a higher yield. Our corn plants grow several stems and have as many as ten cobs per plant. One even had twelve!

☞
[2]

I: That's incredible!

EM: Isn't it? In this way we're building up small-scale self-sufficiency farming. It's much easier and more productive than everyone slogging away on their own and is more fun as well.
Well, I'll work another hour here and then I'll go back home.
I wish you a good time. Good-bye!

He stands up and goes back to one of the rows of potatoes.
And me? I'm a little bit wiser – and even more impressed.
I decide to go back and buy some fruit on the way.
When I cross a street, I suddenly see two cars driving through a red traffic light one after another. I stop in puzzlement and observe the crossroads. Shortly after, another car comes and simply goes on through the red light. It even drives more slowly, consciously feeling its way over the crossroads in spite of the red light. Well I never! I look around to see whether there might be a sign but can't see one.
Then I speak to a young mother who is walking along the street with a pram and holding a little boy by the hand.

I: Excuse me, do you know if this traffic light is out of order?

M: No, why? It's working!

I: But cars keep driving on when it's red.

M: Well, they certainly only do that when the street is clear, don't they?

I: Yes, but ...

M: They're probably drivers with green driving licences.

I: Green driving licences?

  The little boy pulls his mother's arm and urges her to go on.

M: Come with me for a short distance. I've promised the children to go to the town park with them and I can explain it to you on the way.

I: With pleasure, thank you.

M: By the way, I'm Maria. You aren't from here?

I: No, I'm not. My name's Thomas.

M: You know, we don't just have one driving licence for everybody, regardless of how well or badly they drive. Depending on driving practice, skill and frequency of accidents there are several classes of driving licence differing in colour.

I: Aha!

M: Someone who can drive better needn't keep to the prescribed rules so strictly.

I: And that works?

M: Yes, why not? A driving licence with greater freedom is also taken away much sooner if something happens. The responsibility is greater and you have to prove it continually.

I: And so they're simply allowed to drive through a red traffic light?

M: Yes, if the traffic situation permits.

I: Are they also allowed to exceed speed limits?

M: Yes, depending on the situation. That's why there's a little explanation beneath nearly every speed limit sign here.

I: Yes, I noticed that.

M: When it says "Noise" the speed has nothing to do with the traffic situation and should not be exceeded in principle out of consideration for other people.
But if it doesn't say anything, it always means a dangerous bend and then it depends on the car, the weather and the driver's skill how fast they can actually take the bend.

I: That makes sense. Aren't there any speed checks here?

M: Only sporadically. The drivers don't serve as an extra source of income for our towns. Road safety is first and foremost with us and that anyway always depends on the situation. Most accidents happen when the driver is distracted and not concentrating on driving. A lack of attention can't be compensated for by a speed limit, however strict it may be.
Let the driver drive a few kilometres faster; the main thing is that they are fully concentrated and considerate and react quickly to the road situation concerned.

We have now arrived at the park. The girl is sleeping deeply and soundly in the pram. The boy has been impatient the whole time and now at last he can run ahead to the new playground.

I: Aren't you afraid for your children if everyone drives through red traffic lights here?

M: No, the crucial thing is what their parents have taught them. Children should learn to recognise a possible source of danger and assess the potential danger correctly themselves. A traffic light can't do that for them.
That's why it's also nonsense that everyone has to wait at a red light even if no car is within sight, just to show children a good example. Our children rather grow up with the awareness that the traffic lights are not a substitute for one's own attentiveness and caution but a support, and like that everything works better.

She stops for a moment, detects her son in the distance on the playground and checks on her sleeping daughter in the pram.

We are standing in the middle of a magnificent park. It is well looked after and very clean: there is no litter and I can't even see a cigarette end.

Some distance away I see some free areas, where a group of young people are working on something.

I: What are those people up to?

M: They're people from the Academy. They've set up some experimental areas and are testing the growth of fruit and vegetables with the help of new or also traditional or forgotten methods of cultivation. That's interesting, even if sometimes rather curious.

I: In what way?

M: Well, there are, for instance, two experimental areas for potatoes. One is planted normally with potatoes, the other is furnished with wires in the earth as well and equipped with a huge antenna. That has something to do with natural energy fields and Earth's magnetic field. I don't know more exactly but they have put up an informational display there.

I: And they do that quite simply here in the town park?

M: Yes, this is the perfect place – a central public learning and show garden. Everyone meets here and can directly experience what is happening each day.
      Some of today's methods of cultivation in the Kingdom have been tested and improved here and take us further and further in the direction of self-sufficiency.

When we get closer to the playground, a boy aged about seven – obviously Maria's son – runs up to her and tells her full of excitement what he has been building with his dad and that he must show it to her. Right behind him comes a man in his mid-thirties, probably the dad, and greets her affectionately.

D: Hallo darling. Well, is the little one asleep?

And he adds, looking curiously at me:

D: And who have you brought with you?

I: Hallo, I'm Thomas,

 I introduce myself.

I: I'm exploring the town and Maria was able to answer some of my questions.

D: That's good. I'm Paul. And how do you like it with us?

I: Very much. It's very interesting and, above all, a lot's new for me.

D: Yes, Talweis has really come on in recent years. Most people have no idea because they didn't grow up here but five years ago Talweis was a dying town. Before the changeover there was almost nothing here, hardly any industry, commerce or work, There was a little agriculture but it didn't bring in much money. Earnings were meagre because there was so little work. Many people worked elsewhere for weeks or even months. Many commuted every day by car at great expense as the trains didn't stop here anymore. It was important for them to at least be able to sleep with their families.
Intelligent people moved away as did a lot of my friends. I was one of the few who was doing well. I had a secure job with the Inland Revenue, which is the reason I stayed. Then came the changeover and that was a miracle for all us.

M: But you didn't see it like that then.

D: Yes, that's true. At that time I voted against the changeover. But that was because of my fear of change. Inland Revenues offices wouldn't be needed anymore. Of course a certain security was lost after years of being used to the status quo. But nobody sees it like that anymore today after all we've achieved in Talweis.
Today we see how little administration leads to so much development. And if you used to be employed by the public sector, you wonder what you actually toiled for year in and year out. Lawyers and doctors today really have the chance to assure true justice or health. The serious and honest among them have sought further training. Those who were only interested in raking in money have moved away. Nobody sheds any tears over their departure!
Together everyone here can earn their living through the many

offers available – without much effort. Everybody here has more time to really live – according to their very own standard, without financial pressure, without fear of not making ends meet.

I: And what do you do today?

D: My work has become much more comprehensive and interesting. Most of us in the Inland Revenue were taken over by the state sector to convert existing enterprises to the new system.
   Today I work for the state enterprises, do their revenue-expenditure surplus calculation and advise on optimising the business processes. That's a nice task for me – and naturally much more positive than what I used to do. At last I can do something for people and not against them. Although I had always persuaded myself that I was collecting taxes for the public – as was propagated in society –, it looked quite different in daily life. In so many individual cases I was able to close my eyes less and less to the fact that I was working against people and not for them. In addition, there were internal instructions about what to do in particular cases, which no longer had anything to do with the citizens' good. That put an increasingly heavy load on my conscience.
   In this respect I was relieved in the truest sense of the word when the changeover was accomplished and I was offered these positive new tasks. Now I really work for the public, but not by taking money out of their pockets but by helping to optimise processes and reducing costs, thus generating more profit for the state coffers.

At this moment his son comes back and urges him to stop jawing at last. There is still so much to do.

D: Yes, now I have to apply myself to my actual occupation for today again. You can come and have a look at our major project.

We go round the corner to a side-path and an area opens up where a whole crowd of craftsmen, hobbyists and voluntary helpers are working with their children on an adventure playground that some amusement parks would advertise with as their main attraction. A huge castle with towers, ramparts and gates, climbing walls and bars, secret passages, drawbridges and rope bridges, spitting gargoyles and trick fountains, slides, swings, sandpits and so on and so forth are being constructed here.

D: We started this last year and because we are constantly having new and better ideas, we still aren't finished. And it's now got a little bit bigger than planned!

I am impressed – not only by the construction but by the large number of people who are lending a hand together here and building something with fun and joy. Roundabout a little party for young and old has been organised as a picnic on the grass, with coffee, tea, cocoa, milk, cake, biscuits and fruit.

I: Do you pay for all the building material yourselves?

D: No, we don't. The wood comes from the town forest and is provided by the forest official after the project has been examined and considered to serve the public good. It is sawn into pieces of the required size in a state enterprise. My friend Karl is a carpenter with his own business and makes a lot available here, including his know-how.

Supporters provide anything else that is lacking. Last year someone even came and looked at things and was so pleased about what we were creating that he donated 1000 marks.

I: Wow, does something like that often happen?

D: Not such a large amount, but because we have also published this project on the website of the Office for Mutual Support there are a lot of people who make contributions. That's why we have so much money that we have been able to expand our original tower into a whole castle.

I: Well, you certainly have plenty still to do!

D: Yes, yes, but the act of building in itself is already part of the project's success. As the saying goes, the journey is the reward. That's probably why it's taking such a long time. A lot of people actually don't want the castle ever to be finished – especially the children. We are all having such fun building and learning such a lot that we would really miss these afternoons.

I: Well then, I don't want to keep you anymore. Thank you very much indeed for your time and the interesting information. Take care!

D: Yes, all the best to you, too.

M: And enjoy the rest of your time in Talweis!

I stand a while longer and watch what is happening. Then I go on towards the centre of town.

After a while I come to a large supermarket and decide to buy something to eat. At first I have difficulties in finding out where the entrance is as there are check-outs where people come out and check-ins where they go in as well. Then it becomes clear to me that the check-ins at the entrance are in fact weighing machines. Many customers bring their empty containers with them and these first have to be weighed and marked. Others just go in with their containers. I understand the sense only later during my shopping. In many areas there are no shelves with packed goods but large dispensers from which the customers can fill the goods into the containers they have brought with them. Flour, noodles, nuts, grains, dried fruit, muesli and also liquids, such as oil, honey or cleaning products and cosmetics are offered without any packing. Fruit and vegetables are also all loose without packing.

However, I now have a problem as I do not have a container with me. But I very quickly see that unbreakable reusable containers in a variety of shapes and sizes are offered for sale in some places. The weight of the empty container is even stamped underneath these containers. This also explains the people who simply went in without weighing. In addition, bags made of recycled paper are offered, which can help solve my problem.

But there are also a lot of shelves with packed goods as I am used to in other supermarkets. There I rediscover the various coloured crowns, which I am familiar with from the restaurant. Further, I also find black dots and seals resembling stamps and bearing a number. That interests me. The seals are mainly on products I am familiar with but I cannot make any sense of it. So I look for a shop assistant and ask her:

I: Excuse me, may I ask you a quick question?

SA: I'll be glad to help you. Are you looking for something?

I: No, not directly. It's my first time here and I'm surprised at the many different symbols and stickers on your products. Could you explain what they mean?

SA: Yes, of course. The tax stamps are what you see most often.

She points to one of the seals.

SA: They're stuck on products which are taxed and show that the tax has been paid.

I: I thought there wasn't any tax here?

SA: That isn't quite correct. Taxes can be imposed on products that harm the environment or health. Through these taxes the manufacturer has to beforehand pay the money which later has to be spent to remedy probable damage to health and the environment. This prevents a firm which brings harmful products on to the market from making profit but leaving the community to remedy the damage. Today in most countries the government – and hence the taxpayers – or the medical insurance funds – and hence their members – pay for the damage.
In the Kingdom such products aren't made at all anymore and so only articles from outside are affected. And the manufacturers outside aren't subject to our legislation, which is why they don't have to pay these taxes either. But the law says that these products are only allowed to be sold with the taxes imposed. That's why the importer or the seller has to pay these taxes and that is done with these tax stamps. The importer buys them at the Reichsbank and sticks them on the goods so that everyone can see the obligation to pay tax has been met.

I: That does sound complicated. How is it all controlled?

SA: It isn't that complicated at all. These articles aren't bought very often anyway. Because of the tax they have simply become too expensive and now we have very good alternatives that are harmless. The control is in principle carried out by anyone who gets such a packet in their hands and the Reichsbank also makes sporadic checks. But the most important thing is that everybody acts on their own responsibility according to the principle of trust, thus ensuring that strict controls are not necessary at all.

I: Okay, thank you. Then this black dot is still new to me.

SA: It says something about the repacking. In the Kingdom we are increasingly switching to compostable packing materials. This packing here, for instance, is made from corn starch and is fully

compostable. All goods that are still repacked in non-composta-
ble materials have to be marked with a black dot so that the customers can make a conscious decision on their purchases.

The same applies to the ingredients. As the government's obligation to promote health is laid down in the Constitution, a list of
non-hazardous ingredients – the golden list – has been published.
If a food only contains substances from this list, it may be marked
with a golden crown.

The green crown says that all components and ingredients originate from the Kingdom and the blue one that manufacturing and
processing were done according to the guideline on laws of nature.

I: Thank you very much for that detailed explanation. How are all
these marks accepted by the customers?

SA: Very well. Most of them are grateful that they can recognise
what is good and healthy quickly and simply – and, above all,
reliably. Hardly anyone reads the detailed list of ingredients. We
can also see from the sales figures that most of the customers use
these marks as orientation.

I thank her again and then continue on my tour of the shop.

On a closer comparison of some products I recognise the really
distinct differences in price between items from the Kingdom, which
have virtually never been made more expensive because of tax, and
imported items, which in spite of everything have to be purchased
with value-added tax and therefore are accordingly more expensive.
The price difference is very drastic on everything bearing a tax stamp.
It is absolutely clear to me that hardly anybody buys these products
alone because of the price. That is certainly also intended to be a
side-effect.

At the check-out everything goes as usual, except that with the containers the customers have brought with them the weight of the empty
container registered at the check-in is deducted from the total weight
so that only its contents are effectively charged. It does not take long
with me. I have only bought a few fruits and a bottle of juice.

When I am outside again, I at once start eating the strawberries I
have bought. I am now really hungry.

Next to the supermarket there is a service station, as is often the
case. When I look at the prices I cannot believe my eyes. Super only
costs 80 pfennigs a litre and diesel as little as 50 pfennigs. I calculate

several times and can well understand the petrol price. There is no value-added tax and no petroleum tax. But the diesel price is still lower than I can explain to myself.

I go closer to find an answer to this question. Then I see that at two pumps there is another kind of diesel costing 70 pfennigs. As there is nobody at the cash desk at that moment, I go over and ask what the reason is for these two kinds of diesel.

The cashier answers:

C: That's normal diesel and the other is pyrolysis diesel.

I: Aha, and what's the difference?

C: I don't know that either. The pyrolysis diesel is cheaper.

Then another car drives up and I have to end the conversation.

Then I continue on my way. I gradually have to hurry if I want to be at the town council meeting in time, which is my absolute intention. It cannot be much further to the town centre. At two crossroads I ask a passer-by and in a short time I am already back in the familiar town centre.

The town hall is really easy to find so that I get there slightly too early. As I am not acquainted with the customs, I simply wait for the first participants to arrive. I do not need to wait long. Norbert is also one of the first. He sees me and comes over.

N: Hallo, did you find it easily?

I nod.

N: Come with me. We'll go straight in.

I follow him on to one of the upper floors of the town hall, where we enter a large room with dark wood panelling. There is a row of tables with chairs in a U-shape and behind it several rows of chairs. At the front there is another table with three chairs and at the side next to the entrance door there are glasses and drinks.

The town councillors sit down at the row of tables. There are no divisions or departments to be seen, as is normally the case for the different parties. The rows of chairs behind are for guests. I take a seat behind Norbert and watch what is going on. There is a lot of interest. The second and third rows of chairs are almost completely occupied.

Then another three women arrive and all sit down at the table at the front.

Norbert whispers to me:

N: The fair-haired woman is the mayoress and the other two are the keepers of the minutes.

The mayoress opens the meeting, greets all those present and reads out the agenda. Then she announces that twelve new citizens joined the town a week ago. She reads out a list of the names of the people who have passed the citizen's examination.

Citizen's examination? It is now impossible for me to ask Norbert without disturbing the meeting. So I grab a piece of paper and begin making a list of questions I want clarifying later.

There is no response to the question as to whether any additional items should be added to the agenda. Therefore they start working through the agenda topic by topic.

The first topic is a sports and events hall which burnt down recently. Concerning this there is an enquiry from the Reichsbank about the damage or the costs of reconstructing it and if this is actually planned. For as the sports hall was financed by the Reichsbank, the latter may have to reduce the money supply again. As I understand it, money was created for building the hall. But as the equivalent value no longer exists, the money supply has to be readjusted accordingly.

That is not completely clear to me. Therefore it becomes the next point on my list.

Then there is an extensive topic about the budget. An elderly gentleman gives a lengthy explanation about this, including a review of the past years. The town obviously became free of debt a short time after the changeover and since then its revenues have grown continually so that revenue cuts have already been made twice.

In the last few years more state enterprises have become well established and the number of employees has also increased so that the earnings from the German Health insurance fund and the German Pension pensions fund have increased. At the same time the results of the health information programmes and the guidelines for food manufacturers have become noticeable, leading to a perceptible decline in expenditure for German Health. All that together is now to occasion a further cut in earnings. He proposes lowering the charges for water and electricity from the public utilities. There follow endless figures, which I cannot really understand.

There are virtually no counter-arguments to this proposal, so the corresponding motion is adopted unanimously.

The same gentleman speaks again on the next topic. It is about a mosque which is to be built in the town. The question is about whether and in what amount the town should contribute to the building costs. Here the discussion is somewhat more controversial. Some people are in favour of a high contribution as religious pluralism is good for the town and it also contributed to the building of the synagogue. Others think that this issue has to be seen in connection with the whole Kingdom and obviously there is another community which mainly consists of Muslims and has therefore oriented its entire public life very strongly towards Islam, with Friday worship, muezzin, Ramadan, etc. There is a great probability that the majority of Muslims will move there sooner or later and so a mosque is not necessary in the town of Talweis. After some discussion back and forth, it is decided to invite a representative of the Islamic community to the next meeting to obtain concrete information about the financial requirements but also about the probable use of a mosque.

The next topic is about organisational issues concerning the state enterprises in the town. One needs more storage space, another wants to relocate to another site and a third wants to build an extension to its office premises. The town council's opinion is requested and appropriate decisions made on all of these issues.

The last item on the agenda is the motion to reduce the normal working hours by one hour to six hours a day. Since the changeover people's financial burdens have decreased so greatly that they have sufficient income even with shorter working hours. Many have expressed the wish to have more time for their family and social life. Some businesses have already reduced the working hours on their own initiative. A counter-argument is brought forward that such a decision would have a dampening impact on the economic development, for either production would have to be curbed or new employees taken on. Besides that, it would mean that the employees had less purchasing power.

At this point a woman in her mid-40's pipes up and gives a very emotional speech, which I would like to quote word for word:

"Five years after the complete changeover of our economic and political systems, isn't it at last time to say farewell to the growth ideology in our heads as well? Isn't it at last time to recognise that we have so much prosperity with so little work as never before? Why are there still some people who get stomach ache unless such and such a percentage of growth is registered at least? If everyone is doing well, everyone has enough and the firms are working to capacity and are in the black, why for goodness sake do we need more?

Interest no longer has to be paid and there isn't any compulsion to achieve growth on the material level anymore! If we want to grow, then please intellectually, ethically and spiritually. But for this kind of growth we need space and freedom from the pressure of the rat race. And when the rules of our new system make this freedom possible, let us please seize it and make something better out of it than continually recycling and piling up more material."

Loud applause breaks out and almost everyone expresses lively agreement.

In the following vote the motion is adopted with a large majority.

Now follows the report of the regional council, the next higher council. As representative of the town, the mayoress reports briefly on the decisions taken there and gives details of the pending decisions. She requests the town council to vote on each individual decision so that she can vote in the regional council in agreement with the majority opinion of the town council. In this way every community can be heard concerning every single bill in the Kingdom and included in the decision. That is most impressive.

The last item on the agenda is questions from the citizens. A gentleman want to have details about a planned road construction project, an elderly lady asks how far advanced her retirement home is, as she will only be working for one more year. From her question I assume that a house where she will spend her retirement is being built but I also note it on my list of questions. At the end there is a young man who complains that it stinks so strongly of sewerage in a particular street. His complaint is recorded to be forwarded to the office concerned.

Then the meeting is over and everyone is dismissed with a few words of thanks to enjoy their weekend.

I wait until Norbert stands up. He turns to me and says:

N: Well, was it interesting for you?

I: Yes, very, but I have a whole list of questions I would like to discuss.

N: Okay, of course. But I'm fully booked for today. We could have coffee at my place tomorrow afternoon to discuss everything.

I: Fine, if it's all right with you.

N: Sure, no problem. Shall we say 3 pm?

I: That suits me fine.

N: You don't yet know where I live, do you?

He briefly explains me the way to his house, says good-bye and leaves the room with a colleague.

I remain sitting for a while and observe the people. They all make a very open, almost amicable impression on me. At any rate there is absolutely no sign of group or party formations, as I know it from my previous experience.

Suddenly someone taps me on the shoulder from behind. I turn round and recognise Dieter.

"Hallo," we both say simultaneously.

D: Well, what about Monday? Have you thought about it?

I: Yes, I would be very interested in seeing your firm. I would stay an extra night and leave on Monday morning. But then we would have to start right away at 7 am and would only have one hour. Is that possible?

D: Okay, that sounds fine. Let's do it like that. So I expect you at 7 on Monday. Ask Norbert to explain where we are again. See you then!

He weaves his way between the tables and people to the door and vanishes.

I stand up and leave the room as well.

Outside in front of the town hall I notice an unmistakable feeling in my stomach area and decide to eat something. Without hesitating I head for the station to go to *Delicious and Healthy* again. I liked it very much and the food was very good as well.

When I arrive, I am amazed at the crowd there today. The whole place is full. This time I choose some soup and a rice dish and then have to look for a free seat. There is one unoccupied chair at a table for four at the back. I go to it, ask if the seat is free and sit down. The other chairs are occupied by three young people, two of whom seem to be very young to me, maybe still schoolchildren. One of the two women is a few years older. They are having a very lively conversation. I gather it is probably about a project they are all involved in.

Ch: I must have another look at it right afterwards. With the sine law we must be able to get the exact angle, don't you think, Emilie?

says the young man, who is called Christian.
The girl addressed answers:

E: Yes, I think so, but we have time to do it until Monday.

Ch: No, it keeps on bothering me. And we want to cut the beams to size on Monday.

E: If you keep on the pressure like that, the house will be finished next week.

I: You're building a house?

I ask with interest and surprise.

Ch: Yes, so to speak.

E: What do you mean, so to speak? We're building a house as an Academy project.

I: Oh, I see. You're at the Academy.

E: Yes, in the second year of basic studies.

I: And you're building a house?! What exactly are you doing?

Ch: Everything from the architecture and construction planning to the choice of materials and the actual construction, and at the very end we set up a firm to let the premises.

I: Wow! And you are able to do all that?

E: Well, are we able to? We are actually learning everything on the way. Now we are just designing the roof structure and I now understand the actual point of sine, cosine etc. for the first time

I: Yes, that's pretty complicated, isn't it?

E: Strictly speaking, it isn't if you have a concrete example. At school that used to be thrown at us in such an abstract way and we couldn't do anything except learn it by heart. But now our considerations have automatically led us to use all that. Somehow we couldn't get any further and during our research into other possibilities we almost unavoidably came across trigonometry. Lisa helped me a lot with that. She had understood it much better than me at her school.

Lisa is obviously the youngest of the three. She feels she is being addressed and adds:

L: Yes, we did understand its applications at that time. We also already had a small building project at school.

I: Oh, so you were at a different school?

L: Yes, I was. We come from different towns.

E: After school I worked for a few years and didn't decide to study till now.

I: And is that hard?

E: Of the three of us, it's probably the hardest for me. I was in the old school system and first had to completely rethink here.
The first few weeks were awful. First of all, my head was blown empty. We were shown that most of what we had learnt and believed to be reality was really shaky or even directly wrong – only by asking questions or showing contradictions and then by other explanation possibilities. That shook me to the core. At that time I realised how much I had identified myself with my school knowledge. It was almost like a crisis of faith.

Ch: That was normal for us. Lisa and I went to a school in the Kingdom and there nothing was presented as absolute from the beginning and connections were always made to the fundamentals. It was already clear to us that the previous materialistic world view couldn't explain everything correctly and that important dimensions had simply been excluded up to now. I think that also gave you a hard time, didn't it?

he turns to Emilie.

E: Oh yes, it did. That was the second cultural shock for me, so to speak. I come from a world in which everything seems to be clear and explainable and realise here that it was only a small section of reality, which in addition had to work with completely wrong explanations, because it didn't want to recognise the real fundamentals. My goodness, I spent many a sleepless night when I become aware how much I had allowed myself to be misled. As a child I had completely different ideas of so many things, which have now turned out to be right again, but which I had been talked out of during all the years before – until I had believed it all myself.

I: And now you're sure all that's right?

E: No, not at all. But now I know at what point doubt or uncertainty is appropriate and what things are clear and unquestionable. Now I know exactly what something is based on and can thus retrace every theory to its roots. And I know if there are any weak links in the chain. I always used to think everything was sure and unquestionable. Recognising that I had stood on a foundation of sand before was a difficult and sometimes frightening process.

I: And what else have you learnt here at the Academy?

E: A huge amount. I'm really happy that I decided to study here. We got a good introduction to all possible fields of knowledge – mathematics, all natural sciences, geology, astronomy, astrology, law, economics and business management, history, philosophy, psychology, parapsychology – and then …

Ch: You've forgotten medicine,

Christian chips in.

E: Oh yes, that's very important. Not the pretentious medicine but knowledge of health and body. Now I know pretty well how my body works and how I can keep it healthy or make it healthy again. Understanding how disorders can be remedied gives enormous security.
Yes, and then we also have acquired very practical knowledge of music, sport – which is actually part of body science – and crafts, such as woodwork, stone carving and metal work.
And as I said, we're now building a house with all the crafts, including bricklayer, carpenter, roof tiler, plumber, electrician, floor tiler, joiner, etc. etc. etc. … It's really incredible how much you can learn in two years.

Ch: And what fun it is!

Christian adds.

I: And what are you planning to do after your studies?

E: I'm going to apply for a job with the state. As Academy gradu-ates we already have the promise of such a position. Perhaps I'll have a managerial position in a state enterprise.

Ch: I'm going to set up my own business. I have a few business ideas and I'll soon have all the tools to manage a business.

I: And you?

I turn to Lisa, who seems a little more shy.

L: I'm going to continue studying at the Academy.

I: In which direction?

L: Paraphysics.

I: Aha, what can I imagine that to be?

L: Well, if you free magic and parapsychology from all the ho-cus-pocus you come to a natural science that we call paraphysics.

Ch: Lisa has a very strong medial disposition. For that reason she also received a scholarship from the Academy. That is strongly promoted in the Kingdom.

I: And how did you finance your studies?

Ch: In my case my parents paid for most of it. I earned some extra money with a few jobs.

E: And I worked for a few years and saved money for my studies.

I: You don't all come from Talweis?

"No," Christian and Emilie say simultaneously, while Lisa nods her head.

L: Yes, I do.

E: I don't even come from the Kingdom.

I: Oh, really? Did you come here especially for your studies?

E: Yes, I did.

I: And do you want to stay here?

E: Definitely. There's no way I want to go back to the old system.

I: And you?

I turn to Christian.

Ch: I come from a little community in the Kingdom, in Wendland.

E: Where anarchy prevails,

Emilie chips in with a laugh.

Ch: Don't make fun! Yes, our community professes anarchy.

I: I beg your pardon? Anarchy in the Kingdom? That's a contradiction in itself.

Ch: No, not at all. The only reason we even changed over to the Kingdom was that we have the possibility to be autonomous here.

I: You have to explain that to me.

Ch: Of course. According to the Constitution, every community has the right to administer itself without being integrated into a regional body. That means we do our own thing, administer ourselves in our town council, without regional council, district council, etc. and are thus largely autonomous.

I: And the King and the Constitution?

Ch: They don't disturb us. The Constitution anyhow only expresses what we also agree with so we can well accept it and the King is only the guarantor of the Constitution.

I: Then what's different from other communities with you?

Ch: Well, for instance, we have an unconditional basic income for every member of the community. We don't have or want any churches of any religion. We take our decisions according to the principle of unanimity, meaning that all the town councillors have to agree. We want to live real complete equality of all people in practice.

I: What do the other people in the Kingdom think about it?

Ch: Some of them don't find it so good, as you saw before from their reaction.

He points to Emilie.

Ch: But it's accepted.

Emilie interrupts him with a protest.

E: You know I didn't mean it like that! I accept it completely. It's just a bit curious and that's why we sometimes joke about it. I wouldn't want to live like that but I don't have to either.

Ch: Exactly. We don't disturb or influence anyone. The people who would like to live like that move to us and so we are among ourselves and live our way of life and the others live their way of life. It's quite simple.

I: And are you going back there?

Ch: I'll see,

he says with a strange look at Lisa.

Ch: I haven't decided yet.

E: And where do you come from?

Emilie turns to me.

E: Judging by your questions you haven't been here long.

I: Yes, you're right. I've been here just one day.

E: Oh, that really isn't much.

L: But you're going to stay here.

I: Oh, I don't know,

I say uncertainly.

I: I don't have to get to know everything at once. Although I've already seen quite a lot ... What you told me now was almost all new to me.

E: Yes, you can hear and learn a lot of new things here. But you don't really experience the difference to the old system unless you are here for a long time.

You get a different attitude to life, a different relationship to your fellow humans and a different self-image. The changed state rules have a much greater impact than you can imagine up to now. It's like a release, an awakening …

I can't really explain it to you. You may have already realised that people here are in a different mood, that everything here is somehow more humane, but to be really able to grasp that inwardly you have to live here for a while – and then speak to someone from outside to really become aware of the difference.

She laughs and all the others laugh as well.

Ch: But now we have to go. It was nice to meet you.

The three of them stand up and say good-bye to me almost as if I was an old friend.

I remain sitting for a while and finish eating my food. Somehow I feel strangely moved. Particularly Emilie's final words triggered a resonance in me. The people here are actually different or are they special people who have got together here?

I stand up, return my plate and slowly go back to my hotel deep in thought.

This day has provided me with so many new experiences again that I have trouble in recalling all of them to my consciousness. And each individual experience and each individual part of the puzzle was so new and so profound that it would probably take me some time to digest everything completely.

Having arrived in my room, I get ready for bed, reflect for a while and then lie down in the wonderfully comfortable bed.

Next morning I wake up slightly earlier than the previous day. I am woken by the voices and steps of a large number of people I can hear outside. I jump up and go to the window. In the street a large crowd in sports clothes is running and jogging past the hotel. It looks like a big marathon in which half the town is participating – young and old, men and women, and children as well.

I shower, get dressed and go down to breakfast. The brunette who showed me the room on my first evening is there serving the guests.

W: Good morning! Did you sleep well?

I: Yes, very well, thank you. The bed is really stunning!

W: Yes, we have made a great effort to create all the requirements for a good night's rest.

I: What's the secret?

W: Well, first the mattress. It is made of several layers of natural fibres – straw, wool and kapok. That makes it breathable, without static charge, warm and firm so that the spine can be well extended. The stable base of wooden slats also guarantees that. Then the pillow that optimally supports the head and neck the whole night without being pressed together. And finally the quilt made of natural fibres, which is also breathable. In addition to all that, our entire hotel is energetically harmonised.

I: Very impressive. At any rate the effect is clearly noticeable. I have another question. A big crowd ran past here a while ago. Is a marathon taking place here today?

W: No, that happens every Sunday. It started a few years ago and since then more and more people have been meeting to go jogging on Sunday.

I: Aha, that's interesting!

W: Yes, health consciousness has grown enormously in the last few years. Nearly everyone I know does some kind of sport, pays attention to their body, a proper diet or suchlike.

I: Does that also have something to do with the Kingdom?

W: Yes, of course. Those are the consequences of health information and seminars by German Health. They have generally led to a change in consciousness.

I have put together a plate of food for myself from the buffet and am juggling with a glass of orange juice and a bowl of muesli towards one of the tables.

I: Are those events compulsory?

W: They aren't compulsory, but they're free of charge and there's a reduced medical insurance contribution if you attend them. German Health really lives up to its name. It makes great efforts to improve the population's health. And in the meantime a downright health wave has arisen out of it. You experienced that yourself this morning.

Enjoy your meal.

I: Thank you very much. Ah, before I forget, I would like to stay another night. Is that possible?

W: Yes, no problem. We don't have a new reservation for your room. I'll note it right away. Then you'll also get a reduced rate. The room only costs 25 marks a night from three nights.

I: That's good. Many thanks.

I enjoy my breakfast and then go up to my room again.

There I grab the pile of newspapers I had bought two days before and begin to study them.

I am surprised at the abundance of information I find in them. But there is not only information in the form of news but also commentaries, evaluations and comparison. One paper prints an editorial comment on a lot of reports to assess the reliability or conclusiveness of the report. Another paper even goes as far as printing two reports on one piece of news from different sources or perspectives. While reading, I notice for the first time that a lot of topics which have been in the press for some days have not been so definitely clarified as it otherwise seems in the media. Here you can really understand which aspects are still unclear or which reports need to be regarded with caution or reservation. You can really feel how they are struggling for truth everywhere and nobody wants to present something that is still controversial or uncertain as definite. That is an impressive kind of reporting.

Even in the science section reference is made to scientists who question one or another result of research or comment critically or publish their own results that conflict with other previous published ones. This makes clear how dynamic the scientific process is as well and that in science it is by no means the case that one irrevocable truth after another is found and carved in stone.

One newspaper has a section in which the topics from the previous month are treated again to see what has happened in the meantime.

There, for instance, I read full of astonishment that in the meantime there are quite different findings on the Malaysian airliner MH17 allegedly shot down by the Russians, which clearly question the previous versions. Also concerning the Libyan civil war there is obviously quite different information and facts which I have never heard about before. The picture hitherto conveyed thus has to be replaced by a much more complex one. But in the other media this topic has been treated as concluded for a long time.

I am fascinated. I have never experienced such a kind of journalism. Here the reader is shown openly and honestly what has been found out and what has not, what is considered certain and what not, where there are still doubts and where there are conflicting points of view or information. And again and again I also see corrections of the reports or comments from the previous day, when new points of view have emerged.

That is brilliant! In this way you can regain your confidence in the press and I can absolutely imagine how exciting journalism must be here again. Now it is again a matter of being the first to have new information or being able to supplement or refute old information or of who is more trustworthy and reliable in general. This means that propaganda or standardised filtering of information from above no longer has a chance.

The whole thing is so interesting that due to all my reading I do not notice how late it is until after 2 pm.

I jump up quickly, as I have a date with Norbert for coffee. I must not arrive late. And I should not forget my list of questions either. I quickly change my trousers and hurry out of the room.

He had described the way to me and it is a little outside town. But I had already been in that direction yesterday morning so that it is not completely unfamiliar to me.

Shortly before 3 pm I am standing outside a rather new detached house in a quiet street on the outskirts of the town. The lower part is built of natural stone and the upper part of brick with an overhanging roof beneath which you can walk around the whole house without getting your feet wet. The garden is well-kept but not dandified. I like it as it still looks natural.

I go to the front door and ring the bell. A child's voice calls from inside, then I hear footsteps and the door opens. A petite woman with dark hair, who is obviously in an advanced stage of pregnancy, appears in the doorway.

S: Hallo, I'm Sabine. Do come in!

She invites me to come in with a typical hand movement and I enter the house.

I: Hallo, I'm Thomas.

As I go in, I see that a small girl aged three or four is hiding behind Sabine and cautiously looking at me.

I: Hallo! There's someone else there!

I try to entice her out.
Her little head first of all vanishes really quickly behind her mother's back again, but then she comes out again with a timid "Hallo."

I: I'm Thomas and who are you?

There is no answer.

S: That's Beatrice,

her mother replies in her stead.
At that moment Norbert comes through a door and greets me.

N: Hallo. Nice you're here.

I: Hallo!

We shake hands.

N: Come in, Thomas.

I take off my shoes and follow the three of them into the living room. It immediately strikes me that everything is made of beautiful wood – the coat stand, the doors, the dining table, the chairs, all the shelves and cupboards I can see. There is real parquet flooring. Everything looks very tasteful but still cosy.
We sit down at the table which is already set with everything. There is strawberry cake and cocoa.

I: You'll soon be getting a new offspring, won't you?

The two of them look lovingly at each other.

S: Yes, in two weeks.

I: Oh. Then you've certainly packed your suitcase?

S: My suitcase?

I: Yes, for the hospital.

S: No, in the Kingdom children no longer come into the world in hospital.

I: Where does it happen then?

S: Each of our communities has one or more birth houses. The new souls should be received affectionately and warmly. Births aren't illnesses, after all.

I: But what if there are complications?

S: The birth houses are optimally equipped for everything. And for the really bad cases, which are fortunately very rare, there is the emergency doctor.

N: But we've decided on a birth at home.

I: A birth at home!? My respect! Isn't that risky?

S: No, we have a very experienced midwife. She has attended a lot of home births.

I: I'm sure it wasn't easy to find such a midwife.

S: It wasn't that hard. Since the changeover the number of home births has constantly increased. Now you rather have to make sure that you can find one for the date in question.

I: And the insurance problem? Doesn't it exist here?

N: No, that was just a measure against naturalness in the old system to stamp out home births. That's why the compulsory insurance for midwives was made so expensive that hardly anyone could afford it anymore. German Health does it all here. The birth houses are also supported by German Health. So all that's no problem.

I: That's interesting. What will it be, a girl or a boy?

S: We don't know. We only had a quick ultrasonic scan done and it was too early to detect it.

I: No scan? And what about the risk?

S: Well, we didn't have a scan done just because of the risk! An ultrasonic scan is much too risky for us. It heats the tissue of the embryo in an unnatural way and causes structural destruction in the cell tissue. That means that the risk of disrupted growth, brain damage, heart defects, etc. are enormously increased. We don't want to risk all that. Our midwife can palpate everything extremely well and with her ear trumpet she always knows how the child is.

I: And if there's a genetic defect?

S: The scan can't change anything either. You just know about it earlier and the fear and bad feelings put an extra strain on the pregnancy.

N: Genetic defects aren't examined with an ultrasonic scan either. German Health has a quite different way. With us the preparation for pregnancy starts a long time before conception. For if the father's and mother's bodies, fine metabolism, hormonal balance, etc. function as optimally as possible, the likelihood of such defects is reduced to a minimum. That's why every school-leaver here knows how important it is to ensure your body is healthy before conceiving a child.

I: So you reject any intervention from outside?

S: No, definitely not. That's why we had a scan done. We are in favour of everything that is necessary and above all sensible in view of complete knowledge of natural connections and processes.

N: And this discrepancy is more noticeable concerning the subject of pregnancy and birth than almost anywhere else. But today the roots are established worldwide for a variety of development disorders, diseases, degenerative symptoms on a physical level and even more problems on a mental and emotional level, not to speak of the spiritual field.

I: Do you have experience of delivery methods in the Kingdom?

N: Only to a limited extent as the Kingdom hasn't existed that long. However, the methods don't originate in the Kingdom either.

They're much older and more universal and some have been practised with great success for many decades. Here the Kingdom just provides the legal framework to be able to apply these methods unobstructed and not be forced to take measures hostile to life because of government regulations or social pressure. Here there's even a constitutional right to health and the government has an obligation to promote health.

I: How do you deal with vaccinations?

N: Only people who expressly request them get vaccinations in the conventional sense. We have no routine or compulsory vaccinations, especially not for children.

I: Not for children?

i

p. 139

N: No, heaven forbid! They're especially senseless and harmful for children. When a baby is breastfed by its mother, it's protected from infection by its mother. All the same it's become usual worldwide to inject small babies with multiple vaccinations shortly after birth. These vaccines contain aluminium and mercury compounds, formaldehyde and similar strong neurotoxins in amounts that many times exceed the officially permitted maximum doses. That's sheer insanity!
And as the blood-brain barrier, which is the natural mechanism to protect the central nervous system from harmful substances in the blood, doesn't develop until the child is one year old, this causes lifelong damage.

S: And all that's completely unnecessary. If you ensure a healthy pregnancy and a humane and child-friendly birth and breastfeeding time, the baby will be so greatly strengthened alone through these measures that you needn't have any fear of diseases or allergies.

N: At the Academy we've started to re-examine and explore all the open questions about the immune system, diseases and their prevention etc. We'd like to finally close the gaps remaining because research is funded and influenced by business, creating uncertainty everywhere.

At this moment Beatrice has an urgent need to go to the toilet and Sabine hurriedly disappears with her.

We sit silently for a few moments and sip our drinks.

I: You have a really lovely house. How long have you been living here?

N: We moved here two years ago. But we still aren't finished with everything.

I: Did you design it yourselves?

N: Let's say it like this: We made the basic plans but as it was to be a house made completely of mud bricks the statics wouldn't have worked like that. That's why we had to change the plans a bit.

I: Aha?

N: Yes, architecturally you can make pretty well anything with concrete, but with mud bricks you're more limited.

I: I see. Did you regret it?

N: The mud bricks? No, not in the slightest. The living comfort is so agreeable that it's priceless.

I: But wasn't it very expensive?

N: It's correct that the execution and workmanship are indeed somewhat more complex, although not all that much with mud bricks. But a general process of rethinking has started with us in that respect. The long-term benefits simple have more weight. If the inferior building materials which have been used in large quantities during the last few decades, the short lifespan and damage to the environment and the residents' health were included in the calculation, those building materials would be so expensive that nobody would buy them anymore.

I: What do you mean?

N: Well, just take the price of one of your normal new houses. Then you would have to double it to obtain the lifespan of my house. For after that time the normal house would be a ruin and would have to be replaced by a new one. Then add the hospital and medical treatment costs for the residents. For in the following years they'll be exposed to a high level of toxicity from the harmful substances the building materials emit into the indoor air or they become ill from mould. Finally, when the house is pulled down you also have to pay the costs incurred by the disposal of the building materials, which are sometimes harmful to the environment. Then you have the real costs.

I: Okay, I understand. But nobody calculates like that.

N: Yes, we do. You can't get any reasonable financing for such inferior houses here as you can for the high-quality ones.

I: Why is that?

N: Well, the financial institutes in the Kingdom pay great attention to where their money goes. As it is only possible to create money with us when an equivalent added value is created simultaneously, the values created are of crucial importance.

I: I didn't quite understand that.

N: See here! In the Kingdom money is created by the state bank (Reichsbank). That's only permitted when values of common property which are capable of generating added value are created simultaneously.

I: What do you understand by "added value"?

N: For instance, added value is obtained from a building when it's let or when goods are produced in it. The rent or the value of the goods are the added value in that case.
On the other hand, consumer goods, such as food or clothing, can't generate added value. They are simply consumed. No money can be created for them – just as little as it can for values of private property. Money which is already in the bank is used to finance such things.

I: So can bottlenecks arise?

N: No. We only have one bank and so everything people have created is in that bank. The receipts from German Health, German Pension, all the state enterprises and also all the citizens' deposits are in the bank and can be used for financing. Money creation only comes into question if that isn't sufficient. That's very seldom, as you can imagine. Nevertheless, the same assessment standards are generally used for the values created. A long life-cycle and high quality are required everywhere. That has become a basic attitude with us and dealings with money have changed fundamentally compared with the old system. I'm sure you're familiar with sayings such as "If you buy something cheap, you buy twice" or "We aren't rich enough to buy cheap products."

I nod.

N: Poor quality is only an expression of a wrong monetary system and a certain deficiency thinking, which in the end leads to a throw-away mentality. Here we have overcome all that.
This principle of value maintenance and sustainability is also required by the state financial institutions. Therefore each project is first of all examined for quality, sustainability and environmental friendliness before a loan is granted. An inferior building can cause disease or unwellness, and besides that, it doesn't last long. So the Kingdom's financial institutions only grant loans when the requirements to use natural building materials are met and the buildings fulfil certain standards.

I: And who can afford that?

N: A lot of people. Someone who wants to build is loaned money interest-free. Since we have a right to work, there are virtually no unemployed and thus scarcely any failures to repay loans either. But ultimately loans are not absolutely necessary. Someone who works for the community or a state enterprise can live in a rented house or flat at a low rent.

I: There's a right to work? Did I hear that correctly? That's like in the GDR. That inevitably decreases productivity!

N: Yes, you often hear that opinion. But it's very short-sighted. The full employment in the GDR was and still is today laughed at as a waste of money and a productivity killer. But what has been offered as an alternative since reunification? All "unproductive" workers were laid off and since then have received unemployment benefit or social security. However, that means de facto that the people who used to have work and a purpose in life and a task in the community – even if their work may sometimes have been overpaid in relation to their productivity – have now been degraded to receivers of alms. And although the productivity of the other employees has increased, the overall productivity hasn't changed, rather the contrary: with the claimants of long-term unemployment benefit it has decreased to zero and with many others it has now often collapsed as well because of overload, burnout, etc.

Just speak to psychologists and psychiatrists. Then you'll often hear that far more than half the problem cases they have to do with would cease to exist if those concerned had work – and hence a task – again. That's why I find it better to pay people money for their living for any work whatever than give them alms for doing nothing, thus degrading them. The so-called one-euro jobs are probably supposed to go in that direction but were only perceived as an additional abasement by those concerned.

From an economic view it makes no difference in the expenditure whether everybody is enabled to have a livelihood through social security or a right to work. But the second solution at any rate generates something productive for the public weal in return and for those concerned means greater freedom, acceptance and the concrete feeling of being a valuable part of society.

I: Yes, that sounds reasonable. I can understand that.

N: This comparison of the systems is very interesting. After all, we Germans are the only ones to have the possibility of a synthesis from lived experience.

In the GDR there was the right to work. But there were no freedom rights in an economic respect. That's why it was basically not socialism but state capitalism. Because of the government control the economy was no longer creative in the end although it was definitely productive. In the Kingdom we have both – the freedom element as a free market economy and the control element with the state enterprises. The state enterprises primarily have the task of providing and assuring a supply of essentials to the population. If that can be guaranteed by private companies, the state enterprises withdraw.

I: Is this control necessary and sensible then?

N: Definitely. Supplying the population with elementary goods and services assures a certain quality and price standard, which prevents the population from possibly being dependent on poor quality or excessive prices from private suppliers.

For instance, our free public transport ensures that public transport is used everywhere as far as possible, which of course greatly benefits the environment.

Besides that, as a result of the state enterprises there are the same production conditions everywhere. This means that there is almost no necessity anymore to transport goods over long distances. On the contrary, as the additional transport makes them more expensive, this promotes regional industry.

I: I'd like to come back to what you mentioned before – money creation. Does it mean that money is simply printed for particular projects if not enough is available?

N: Yes, when there is a simultaneous creation of value in public property and generation of added value. In return the money supply naturally has to be reduced again when values created are destroyed or broken.

I: Well I never! So money is simply printed here as needed and then withdrawn again!

N: Why are you so astonished about it? Outside in the old system money has been printed for years without being needed, without sense and no matter what the money is used for – simply to keep the sick system going a bit longer. And nothing is withdrawn. Although the money supply has to be regulated again some time as well, that is left to the inevitable total crash, which happens at the expense of ordinary folk.

I: But in both systems the government prints money in the interests of the public so that …

N: Not at all.

Norbert interrupts me.

N: You're quite wrong. In the old system it isn't the government but private banks that print money and why do you think they do it in the public's interest?

I: Well, so that there's enough money to pay the debts.

N: I would rather say: So that there's enough money to run up more debts!

I stare at Norbert blankly.

N: The central banks loan the freshly printed money at interest to other banks and governments. This increases the mountain of debt enormously. And if someone goes bankrupt, the banks become owners of the securities pledged. In this way their real assets increase continually.
At some time or other the economy collapses and then everything belongs to them anyway. But ordinary people lose everything. Even their savings are taken because they lose value increasingly because of inflation.

I: But now let's go back another step. I have always thought up to now that the government creates money and the banks only work with it.

N: Then you're completely wrongly informed. If the government created the money, why would it have debts for which it has to pay interest?

I: So what's the real situation?

N: Well, money is created by the central banks. But today, when most payments are no longer made in cash, all banks can use tricks with the deposits in the accounts to create money quite independently of the central banks. They exploit the fact that only a small part of the money in their customers' accounts actually has to be available as cash or as minimum reserves and use the rest of the existing demand deposits as alleged minimum reserves for loans, which they transfer to their customers' accounts. In this way they lend several times the amount that is really deposited with them.
That's one of the reasons why cash transactions are becoming increasingly restricted. If cash ceases to exist one day, all the barriers will fall for these banks. Then they no longer have to fear a run on the banks. At the moment they wouldn't be able to pay out even 3% of their demand deposits in cash. If more customers wanted that, they would be bankrupt on the spot.

i
p. 151

I: For which case we have the deposit protection fund …

☞ p. 181

N: Unfortunately that's no more than eyewash. For according to the statutes of the deposit protection fund no right exists to claim anything from this fund.

I: What? That can't be true! Then what's the point of the whole thing?

N: It's supposed to reassure people so that there isn't a run on the banks. For that would be the end of all today's commercial banks and thus of the whole financial system.

I: And what's the role of the central banks?

N: The central banks are the institutions that can create physical money, not just bank money. They then lend this money at interest to the commercial banks or the government.
The joke is that everyone thinks they are state or even supranational institutions. But the reality is quite different.

I: How is it different?

N: Well, the Federal Reserve Bank, the US central bank, is a private bank. Shortly before the First World War some high-ranking, influential bankers ensured that their new bank was awarded the monopoly of creating money, with a legally guaranteed 6% dividend after deduction of all expenses and without the government having a right to a say in the matter. Today that is so neatly described as an "exceptional blend of public and private elements, independent of the government."

i p. 155

I: Do you have proof of that? It sounds like another of those "conspiracy theories" to me.

N: There's a whole array of very informative books about it, even including one by Ron Paul, a long-standing Congressman and three-time presidential candidate. Here we can safely speak of a proved conspiracy, if you insist on using that term, but not of a theory.
And while we are on the subject, I'd like to call your attention to a relatively new study by the renowned Princeton University. In this study a professor of politics looked at almost 2000 funda-

☞ [3]

☞ [4]

mental political decisions in the USA during a period of 20 years, for which national opinion polls were conducted and evaluated them statistically. The result was that the opinions of the average American had almost no influence on the decisions, and public pressure groups had little influence as well. A small number of wealthy citizens and influential business organisations had by far the greatest weight. In his concluding sentence the author even seriously questions America's claim to be a democratic society.

This matches a report in the New York Times which says that fewer than 400 families paid more than half the money donated to the electoral campaign for the presidency in 2016. With the Republicans it was even only 130 families.

Do you think that the influence of these families is confined to money?

I: Hm.

I don't know what to say.

I: That doesn't really sound good. I must admit you're right. But we aren't in America after all.

N: You're right about that. But we mustn't forget that the USA has been exerting a controlling influence worldwide for 100 years.

I: How is it with the European Central Bank?

N: The organisational structure is the same everywhere. The ECB is a joint-stock company, just as is the BIS, the Bank for International Settlements, which is virtually the central bank for the central banks. The shares in the ECB are held by the national central banks of the EU and the shares in the BIS by the central banks. Independence in every direction is stressed everywhere, while we should ask ourselves what this independence means and if it is good or bad. Concerning the ECB we also read that it looks like a company at first glance but isn't a company.

The fact is that nobody has an influence on the ECB at a political level. It can do or not do what it wants. Of course it has to report from time to time but that's why it still can do what it likes. There's no democratic influence.

If you know, for instance, that Italy's and Greece's central banks are 100% private and Belgium's 50% and when you see what goes on at the Fed, you naturally may start to have your doubts. In addition, there are quite different connections, which would, I think, go too far. Maybe we should rather come back to the Kingdom.

I: Yes, I agree. How does all that work here in the Kingdom?

N: Our financial sector is just being established completely differently. According to the Constitution, the state exercises sole financial authority: the Royal Reichsbank is the protector of the currency and monitors the money supply by creating money or reducing the money supply; the money supply must always be covered by real values, there are no private banks and interest is forbidden.

I: Yes, we talked about interest in the train. I still can't see it as so dramatic. A low percentage of interest isn't really so bad. And I don't really find it so unpleasant to let money work for you either.

N: The problem is that we don't have any real idea of exponential growth, which is what happens with interest and compound interest. We humans think and live with a linear horizon of experience. We simply lack the imagination for exponential processes. That's why an amount of interest of 275,000 dollars for just one dollar, which I calculated for you, is surprising to everyone.
But I want to show you another example: you may know the old story in which the reward for inventing the game of chess is to be paid in grains of wheat.

I: Yes. I do. One grain on the first square, two grains on the second, four grains on the third and then always the double amount of grains on the next square until the whole chess board is full.

N: That's exactly what I mean. With our linear background of experience it sounds like a banal process with a clear result. But the result of this exponential scheme is an amount of wheat 1500 times exceeding the current annual wheat production of the whole world.

I: Incredible!

N: Yes, unimaginable in the truest sense of the word! You can see that we can't imagine exponential processes and that's why we can't control them either. If you have naively signed a contract with such a process, it can only ultimately end in a collapse.

I: Hm.

N: And this collapse doesn't mean that a particular loan can't be repaid; it affects the system as a whole. We had already spoken about the fact that we all operate with borrowed money in the end. But let me explain that in more detail, quite concretely from the beginning.
When the euro was introduced the central bank, for instance, put one billion euros into circulation – let's say at an annual interest rate of 2%. That means that after one year the ECB will get back one billion and 20 million euros, right?

I: Okay.

N: That's why the banks and all the borrowers – that means all of us – have to make great efforts to earn this money. That's clear, isn't it?

I: Yes, it's clear.

N: But! How are the one billion and 20 million to be repaid if only one billion was issued?

I: Hm.

I think I stare at Norbert like a schoolboy.

N: Do you see? So much money doesn't exist. That's the crux. From the start interest creates a deficiency system, in which the devil takes the hindmost. The last ones can't satisfy the claims anymore and lose the securities they've pledged. This system can only function for a while if new money is issued again and again. The old loans are serviced with new bigger ones – a snowball system!
That's why the interest system encroaches on the consciousness and lives of all of us. We all have pressure and have to toil to make enough profit – with whatever means. And for what?

I am still sitting and staring at Norbert.

N: For the income that someone somewhere has obtained through interest without having to do any work for it themselves. Only for that someone else somewhere else has to do the equivalent amount of work – without getting anything for it.

I am gobsmacked. That is so logical and clear – simply hair-raising.

N: That's why interest is the root of most problems And a fair monetary system is just not possible with interest. We can't back a currency permanently with tangible values when it continues to be inflated by an interest system.

I: What do you mean by that?

N: Well, the (German) word "Währung" (currency) comes from "Gewähr" (guarantee). Money was originally only created to simplify the exchange of goods and services. Theoretically, instead of paying money, we could do the service ourselves or directly obtain the material elsewhere. We pay money to avoid this work – a sensible exchange in our judgement. The amount may be subjective and negotiable. If you're young and energetic, you may prefer to make some things yourself rather than pay a lot of money for them. But if you're old and sick, you are happy that someone does it for you and pay them for it. In any case you have obtained something real in return or a saving through paying a certain sum of money.
But if this money, which you've had to earn yourself through particular work, loses value so that you can't get anything for it some years later, which was actually the reason you earned it, you will have been cheated of getting something in return. And that is the very thing that doesn't happen in the Kingdom. Our money isn't only a mode of payment but a legal mode of payment, i.e. by law each coin and each note offers the guarantee of something in return depending on its value. That means that the money can always be exchanged for something and the value of this thing isn't allowed to decrease. The state with the Royal Reichsbank guarantees this by continually monitoring the backing with tangible values, from the start ruling out the enrichment of a few idle people at the expense of the general population.

i *p. 157*

I: You stress the thing about the currency as if it was something special.

N: It really is. Where else in the world today is there a legal currency, in addition backed with tangible values? Especially in recent
years such excessive amounts of money have been printed everywhere – just like that from nothing without their being matched
by any values.

The euro isn't a currency anymore. You have no right to have
your euro notes accepted by anybody. You can already see that
with 500-euro notes. They are hardly accepted as payment anywhere. And the counterfeiting of euros is only forbidden by the
copyright law. That's why they bear the copyright symbol as if
they were works of art. The euro is still a generally accepted
mode of payment. But that may suddenly change if there is a
crisis.

I: Phew, I think I have to digest that first.

  I take a large mouthful of cocoa.

I: But at any rate I have now probably understood one point on
my list of questions. It was about the topic of the sports hall in the
council meeting.

N: Yes, it was financed by creating money and burnt down two
weeks ago. That's why the Reichsbank now wants to clarify if
the hall should be rebuilt, if financing is necessary, etc. so as to
be able to decide if that has to have an influence on the money
supply.

But what do you think about going out into the garden for a bit.
The weather is actually too nice to sit inside.

I: Yes, that's a good idea!

  We go into the garden and stretch our legs.

I: How does financing actually work concretely with you? You said
you financed your house?

N: Yes, we did. You simply go to the Reichskasse (state financial
institution) and make an application. They have a large number
of experts on hand, who then examine your project and inform
you whether and how much financing they could give you.

I: And what does it depend on?

N: Above all on the sense and value of the project or with commercial projects on the ability to generate added value. If everything
is in order, a loan agreement is negotiated – length of time, instalments, etc. – and then you get the money.

I: Interest-free.

N: Yes, interest-free.

I: How is all the work financed then?

N: There's a handling fee. The examination alone is often very
complex. The costs are covered by the fee.

I: And then you pay your instalments and everything is ready,
without interest …

N: Yes, that shortens the length of time considerably. I will be finished in 12 years. Then I will be free of debt.

I: It's a great thing. And the sustainability of the building, materials, etc., all that is included in the assessment?

N: Yes, it is.

I: What kind of heating do you have?

N: We have a tiled stove on the ground floor that can heat the
whole house. But we mainly heat with electricity.

I: With electricity?

N: Yes, we have concealed wall heating with very flexible infrared
warmth.

I: But electricity is vastly expensive!

N: Actually not. And in a few years it will cost almost nothing.

I: How is that?

N: Some very promising investigations and developments with zero-point energy are going on at the moment. One of our communities already has a major project running. They heat their
greenhouses with it.

I: Yes, I've already heard about it.

N: When it's fully developed, all public electricity will be much cheaper and then such devices are also planned for private consumption. We designed our house on that basis. The tiled stove is actually only for the transition and for rare occasions when we simply want to enjoy the pleasure of a wood fire.

I: Do other people also act like that?

N: People who build new houses do. Although there are still some who install oil heating. Most old houses still have oil heating. During the transition we are using modern manufacturing processes for heating oil and diesel.

I: Is that the pyrolysis I saw at a petrol station?

N: Yes, exactly. Pyrolysis is a process used to crack long-chain hydrocarbons, e.g. from plastic, tyres or suchlike at high temperatures. This process is used on a large scale in one of our communities to produce heating oil and diesel.

I: That's why it's cheaper?

N: Yes, that's why. We have to buy the rest of the petrol and heating oil. Although we get it directly from overseas tax-free, our own production from plastic waste is even cheaper.

I: I still have oil. But I want to switch to CO_2-neutral methods.

N: Oh, don't believe that fairy tale. I wouldn't spend a single mark because of the CO_2 story.

I: What do you mean it's a fairy tale? Global warming is obvious.

i
p. 143
N: But not because of CO_2. If you like, I can refute the theory in a quite simple way understandable to everyone.

I: Okay, go ahead!

N: The argumentation for the greenhouse effect goes like this:
   1. Normal visible sunlight hits Earth's surface relatively unfiltered and heats it. The infra-red-active molecules do not yet play a part here.
   2. Earth's heated surface emits thermal radiation – i.e. infra-red rays – back into space.

3. These infra-red rays are now absorbed by infra-red-active molecules in the air and radiated back to Earth's surface again to a certain extent. Infra-red-active molecules are, for instance, CO_2 and, to a much greater degree water, H_2O.
4. This heats Earth's surface even more.
5. If we now substitute water for part of the air, the same process takes place except that there are many more infra-red-active molecules which radiate back the radiation much more strongly. So the greenhouse effect is greater and the soil beneath is much warmer.

That was it.

I: What do you mean: That was it?

N: Have you ever been to a lake with a sandy beach on a hot summer day? As soon as you go from the hot sand into the water, the sand ought to be even hotter.

I: Why hotter?

N: Well, because the greenhouse effect is allegedly much stronger under water because of the large number of water molecules than it is in the air with the small number of CO_2 molecules.

I: Okay, I understand. That was it.

N: Yes, checkmate in five moves!

I: But there must be a catch somewhere. All the scientists aren't really that stupid.

N: You can make a lot of money with the CO_2 story and exert a lot of public pressure. You just have to inform yourself thoroughly. Then you'll find quite different opinions and scientific investigations as well.

Here at the Academy we ourselves have had a few top-class climatologists. They presented something quite different. Basically Earth is now returning to an old balance from which it was catapulted by natural global disasters a few thousand years ago. It would also be like that if there weren't any humans, cars, factories, heating or cows.

I: And nobody knows anything about it!?

N: Most people here know. We have a different information system from you.

At this moment Sabine and Beatrice come out to us and play on the swing.

S: Well, you two, have you been talking till your heads smoked?

I: I have the feeling mine is smoking.

I reply with a laugh.

I: But it's just very interesting. I'm really glad I have the possibility to get all my questions answered here.

S: Yes, Norbert is also a competent person for that.

I: Why are you actually doing that?

I turn to Norbert.

I: I wanted to ask you that the whole time. I mean, you are taking a great deal of time for me although we have only just met.

N: I simply enjoy doing it. It's fun for me to present our achievements. I'm just proud of our town, our country and everything we've accomplished together in the brief time – and that's why I like showing it to others.

I: That almost sounds like something resembling national pride.

N: Yes, if you want to call it that. Shouldn't a people be proud of its achievements?

I: Well, with us Germans that does have a really bad aftertaste.

N: Because of happenings in our grandfathers' days, and besides that in war times. It's good to be conscious of the past, above all the bad things. But it isn't good when an entire people is still robbed of its self-confidence and its identity 70 years later.

I: What do you mean "robbed of its identity"?

N: We Germans are today generally fastened to the atrocities of the Nazi regime and we even fasten ourselves to them. However, we and our fathers and grandfathers didn't only do bad things. And we were far from being the only ones to have committed atrocities. But we were chosen to be scapegoats for the world, in fact long before World War II, actually already before World War I. There were major powerful international interest groups which ultimately manoeuvred Germany into this position and role. And the Germans cooperated and are still doing so today.

I: What do you mean by that?

N: Well, did you know, for instance, that Hitler and the NSDAP were financed to a large extent by the international banking cartel?

I: Hm, no, I didn't. It sounds like another conspiracy theory.

N: Just like everything that doesn't fit into the picture. So far modern history has always been written from the victorious powers' viewpoint and that's what we learnt at school and internalised.
At the Academy we've started having a fresh, really objective look at everything. It's interesting to see what contradictions and inconsistencies emerge. I think a much more differentiated picture will be revealed when the archives are gradually opened, And that will change the image of us Germans again. But the first thing we have to do is regain our state sovereignty.

I: What's that supposed to mean?

N: Don't tell me you don't know you don't have a state at all!

I: I don't understand ...

N: Sorry. For me it has been clear for so many years that I sometimes completely forget that most people outside still don't know that the Federal Republic of Germany isn't a state.

i
p. 169

I: So what is it?

N: The Federal Republic of Germany is a construction created by the occupying powers after the war so as to be able to administer the occupied country better. It's, so to speak, a firm set up by the supreme commander of the occupying troops – not a state.

I: That can't be true!

N: It is! You're still an occupied territory. There is and has never been a peace agreement nor any valid document under international law which would have determined something else.

I: And the federal government, the parliament (Bundestag) and the Basic Law?

i
p. 165

N: All just part of the administration of your occupying powers but not state structures! The Basic Law isn't a constitution. It wasn't adopted by popular vote. The Basic Law itself says that.

I: Well, I'm absolutely dumbfounded. So what's Germany's legal status then?

N: The German Reich still exists. It wasn't terminated but isn't functional because of a lack of public officers. Unlike the Federal Republic of Germany, the Kingdom of Germany is a correct German state under international law with a valid constitution.

I: And the laws?

N: As the Federal Republic of Germany isn't a state but virtually a firm, it can't pass any laws. It can, so to speak, only make contracts with its personnel. As long as you're a member of the FRG's personnel, which is certified by your identity card (German: personnel identification card), you're subject to the rules established by the FRG.
But even here there are some contradictions. The so-called Federal Constitutional Court has declared the parliamentary electoral system to be in breach of the Basic Law. But this system has been in force since 1957. So all parliamentary elections since 1957 have been in breach of the Basic Law and thus naturally the federal governments and the laws passed, too. But in spite of that these laws continue to be applied.
Furthermore, laws passed between 1933 and 1945 are still applied. But after the capitulation of the German armed forces (Wehrmacht) the allies declared these laws to be void.
Legally it's an utter mess. That's why real constitutional legality isn't formally possible at all.

I: Why doesn't anyone know that?

N: Oh, in the meantime a whole lot of people know. You only need

to search on the internet, for instance, in Dun & Bradstreet's ☞
directory of firms and find the FRG there under the firm name p. 181
"Federal Republic of Germany" with a firm number and the whole
set-up.

Incidentally, there you will also find the Deutsche Bundesbank
(German central bank) and the ECB and the Fed, to come back
to the subject we were talking about before.

I: Oh, was that what you meant before when you said it would go
      too far?

N: Yes, it is. When the FRG, which is a firm and not a state, man-
      ages a "state" bank, the Deutsche Bundesbank, which, in its turn,
      holds a share in the ECB, who does all that ultimately belong to
      and who really has the say?

I: Yes, now I understand. But I don't understand why they simply
      put up with it.

N: In fact the authorities are just continuing as if nothing had hap-
      pened. When someone points out the real legal situation, they
      ignore it. The system simply uses its factual power and later when
      the court bailiff is standing at the door with an enforcement no-
      tice, the fee, fine or whatever always has to be paid even though
      there never was a real legal foundation for it.
      But I'd say we should go inside again.

  It is gradually getting chilly and so we go back inside to the sofa.
Sabine brings us some more drinks and we continue our highly interesting conversation.

I: So the FRG isn't a constitutional state?

N: From the point of view of international law the FRG isn't a state
      and so any laws it has passed and operates with are void. But it
      doesn't even keep its own laws. You wouldn't believe what we
      sometimes experienced before the FRG virtually recognised the
      Kingdom. They used all possible means to destroy the project.
      First everything was hushed up. When interest in it showed a
      continual increase, it was ridiculed. They set up a special internet
      portal which slagged us derisively, sarcastically and polemically.
      The aim was simply that nobody should dare to profess the thing

openly because they would fall victim to public mockery.

But when that didn't work either, they took drastic measures. Huge police platoons came and made raids with flimsy court orders and first of all seized everything they could get hold of. They weren't much bothered if it was legal or not. The aim was not justice but destruction. They hoped that such operations would be a sufficient deterrent so that any court decisions would finally not be relevant anymore – according to the motto, when everything has been destroyed, we can perfectly well apologise for our breaches of the law.

I: And you still kept going?

N: Yes, not only that. The greater the reprisals, the more support and backing we received from the public. And then finally, when our town had changed over to the Kingdom, they couldn't do anything anymore.

I: How did you manage it?

N: The changeover?

I: Yes.

i
p. 163

i
p. 167

N: Well, actually it's a relatively simple process. any community can do it. In Europe we have the principle of subsidiarity, which means that all responsibilities of public administration can be assumed by the lowest level of organisation and even should be unless it involves considerable difficulties. The lowest level is the community. Besides that, replaceability of the government and its responsibility to the representatives of the people are constitutional principles of the FRG laid down in the criminal code.

We applied these two principles and put forward a motion in the town council to replace the government for our town and decide on a new government for ourselves, i.e. that of the Kingdom. That was first of all rejected by the town council but led to discussions and considerable interest in the population.

Our town was heavily in debt at that time and there were also strong citizens' initiatives for a new school with the Shetinin system and for environmental measures because of a factory in the town. That's why we saw a good chance of winning a majority in the population for the project and so we organised a collection of signatures for a petition for a referendum.

I: And you managed to push it through?

N: Yes, the referendum was held and the majority of the people entitled to vote voted in favour.

I: And then you simply said good-bye to the federal government and the FRG?

i
p. 177

N: So to speak. Of course it went back and forth for a while but the legal situation is now regulated. If an existing community as a regional public body makes use of its rights according to the principles of the Constitution, you would have to act as an open dictatorship to stop it.

i
p. 167

In this case some things would also take effect which Peter had always talked about but which we haven't really experienced until then ...

In reply to my questioning look he adds:

N: Peter is our head of state.
He stressed from the beginning that it isn't a matter of demonising or fighting the existing system but of building up something new and better that can one day supersede the old system. He even always said the existing system was the best we had had so far. It had brought us peace and prosperity – and created the possibility of building up something new absolutely legally in harmony with the existing laws. This peaceful changeover to a new system, which we've now accomplished here, was obviously intended.

I: Intended?

N: Yes. Just look at the repeated references to the provisional character of the Basic Law or the FRG as a structure similar to a state. The fathers of the Basic Law didn't want a constitution or a state; they wanted to leave the door open for a major holistic renewal. Also the subsequent governments have again and again built appropriate possibilities into the laws.
If it wasn't the case, we wouldn't have been able to accomplish a peaceful legal changeover.

I: And why was and is there so much opposition then?

N: Because a lot of people have meanwhile identified themselves with the existing temporary arrangement and don't want any more change. Above all, the middle and junior civil servants, who themselves don't have an overview of the circumstances, are the ones who have caused us trouble. Paradoxically, that didn't happen by their keeping to the existing laws but by their breaking them.

At the level of senior management some have been positively inclined towards us for a long time. Peter has always emphasised that. At the Federal Agency for Financial Market Supervision (Ba-Fin), the extended arm of the banking cartel of the elite family clans, there were certainly some who were aware that our project was positive. But they were stuck in their structures and bound by instructions.

But otherwise those at the top are equally aware of the deplorable state of affairs and wrong development and even in America some people are seeking a solution for Germany's untenable status but don't know what to do.

Maybe it's Germany's task to initiate a renewal for others as well. After all, the Germans are the only ones in Europe who aren't bound by the EU agreements.

I: Why's that?

N: Because they haven't been ratified by an internationally legitimate German government or representative of the people.

I: You mean because the FRG isn't a state?

N: Yes, that's what I mean. So we Germans have the legal possibility of rethinking and tackling the problem of the entire construction of the EU, which many people now perceive rather as a nightmare – not only for ourselves but for all Europeans.
       That reminds me of a sentence written by a philosopher in the 19th century: "The thorough Germany cannot revolutionise without revolutionising from its foundations up. The emancipation of the Germans is the emancipation of humanity" (Karl Marx).
       That was in a different context at that time but maybe the sentence is today more valid than ever.

☞
[5]

I: So you attach more global importance to the whole thing?

N: Yes and no. The whole direct importance is the welfare of the citizens in each community, as it is with us in Talweis. But if that works and we thus prove how things can be different and better, why should it stay limited to our town or country?

The current refugee problem shows how wrong and short-sighted politicians have been to be only concerned about welfare at home, thereby disadvantaging, exploiting or even harming others.

Peter hasn't already written a Charter for the Renewed United ☞
Nations for nothing.   [6]

I: What was Peter's role in the whole process?

N: Peter was the real initiator of the whole project. Years ago he had the vision and also had a profound knowledge of the legal situation with all its loopholes and tricks. I believe he knew paragraphs that scarcely anyone before him had read correctly.

I: Is he a lawyer?

N: No, that's just it. He's a totally self-made man. But he had the right instinct and above all unshakeable confidence in himself. Somehow he seemed to know all that was right and it was now time for it and he would make a success of it. That gave all of us a lot of energy and optimism, even at times when hardly any light was to be seen on the horizon.

He had the courage to plough over new ground in the FRG by provoking a whole series of court proceedings to be able to have various things clarified by the court. In doing this, he often stood with more than one leg in prison. But ultimately the many court cases made it possible to achieve legal security regarding our projects in the FRG as well. We really have a lot to thank him for in that respect.

I: But isn't it a bit too egocentric that he had himself crowned king?

N: He didn't do that at all! He'd actually planned a democratic republic of councils and wanted to realise it with another legal possibility. In fact he tried to found a public corporation, which would have built up its own internal legal and organisational structures quite legally under FRG law. In this way it would have been able to create its own system with its own real offices and even levy its own taxes. This structure would not have been assailable under

FRG law either. But for that project he would have needed at least 80,000 members, which is why it failed.

I: It failed because 80,000 members couldn't be found? Judging by everything I've seen and experienced here, I can't imagine that in a country of our size it wasn't possible to get at least 80,000 people enthusiastic about it?

N: Yes, but that was why it failed. At that time people couldn't imagine it. As much as Peter would have liked, it wasn't possible to find more than a thousand.

Of course Peter could have gone on working on it for a few years but he felt considerable time pressure because of the economic situation, which was becoming increasingly threatening. If a euro crash or a collapse of the world economic system had happened without there being a functioning alternative structure, everything would have sunk into chaos. And creating a new system from chaos is extremely difficult.

And so with a heavy heart he finally decided to found the state with the few people who were there. It wasn't possible to think of an ascending system of councils with town councils, regional councils and district councils up to the state council because of the lack of people. However, a government was necessary to meet the criteria for a state. That was how the idea of a Kingdom came into being. Although we're a democracy, as the king is essentially only the representative head of state, government is assumed by a Supreme Sovereign until the entire system has been completely built up and Peter was elected to this office by the founding sovereigns.

i
p. 161

I: So he isn't the king and didn't crown himself either.

N: Exactly.

I: That's extremely interesting.

But, while we're talking about law, what about justice and courts with you? I mean, there will be problems ending up in court again and again here as well …

N: Yes, of course. Some misunderstandings and differences of opinion which can't be resolved in another way can always arise. There are some people who have become accustomed to tricking others at the latter's expense their whole lives and they get into contentious situations again and again.

But in general the number of court cases has decreased drastically. In addition, the proceedings themselves have also become shorter and less complicated.

I: What's the reason for that?

N: The main reason is the new understanding of justice. The highest principle with us is that justice is above written law. That means that with everything that is done and decided it is a question of justice and not of interpreting paragraphs.

Most of your court disputes are about paragraphs which one person interprets in one way and another in another or paragraphs which one person didn't know about but the other uses cleverly to their advantage, according to the principle that ignorance of the law is no excuse. If it leads to injustice, such paragraphs aren't ultimately decisive with us.

I: So where is the predictability of legal decisions if you can't rely on the paragraphs at all?

N: Legal certainty lies in the consciousness of being just and acting lawfully. Paragraphs can be a certain pointer in this. But you can't use paragraphs to cover every possible situation. However, that's what legal experts have tried to do during the last few centuries and they haven't produced anything but a vast mountain of paragraphs that one person alone can't know. That hasn't resulted in greater legal certainty but rather the opposite.

There are constantly incidents which are quite clearly unjust to everyone although they are completely consistent with the paragraphs and therefore make an additional paragraph necessary to regulate an exception.

I: Oh yes, I know plenty of those.

N: That's why contract law has also been placed on a completely new footing. We have put an end to the vast agreements which attempt to provide a paragraph for every conceivable contingency and then in the end one of the parties finds a tiny loophole or a cleverly constructed scheme which they can use to shortchange their contractual partner quite "legally."

I: I even know cases where those loopholes were deliberately built into the agreement when it was drawn up.

N: Exactly. And if the other party doesn't think just as connivingly and signs the agreement, they have fallen into the trap.

I: And how do you go about it?

N: With us a contract in principle consists of only three clear parts: In the first part one of the parties describes what objective they are striving for in the agreement, in the second part the other party does the same and in the third part they both confirm with their signature that they undertake to realise the other party's desired objective and what means they intend to resort to.

I: Is that all?

N: Yes, it's as simple as that. How the two of them approach the matter isn't important at all as long as both of them have realised their desired goals at the end and are satisfied.

I: And if that isn't the case?

N: If that isn't the case, the dissatisfied party will naturally first demand that the other meet their obligations. If the latter thinks they did everything correctly, the dissatisfied party can go to court. And there the status quo achieved is simply compared with the result striven for and contractually agreed by the two parties. The deficits are elaborated and the court examines whether the other party is responsible for the dissatisfied party's deficit or if there are independent reasons for it. The judge then decides on the basis of this.

I: Incredible!

I am really speechless at how simple it is.

At the same time I have to think of contracts I have concluded. Some had so much small print that I did not read it at all. Although I did read the small print in others I still did not really know what I was actually signing then.

Suddenly I notice that Sabine and Beatrice are not there anymore. They must have left the room during our conversation.

A glance at my watch makes me feel really uneasy.

I: It's really become late. I don't want to steal all your Sunday.

N: But you had noted more questions. We can go through them before you go.

I: Yes, that's right. Most of them have been answered in the course of our conversation, but there are still a few left.

   I rummage around for my list and go through it.

I: Oh, yes! In the council meeting yesterday they mentioned people who had passed a citizenship examination. What does that mean?

N: That's relatively simple. In the Kingdom there are three classes – people, citizens and deme. Although the higher ranks are open to everyone you have to qualify for them.

I: What do the classes mean?

N: They express the degree of commitment to the community. Citizens and deme have active and passive voting rights.

I: Does that mean that none of the others are allowed to vote?

N: Yes, until they have passed the citizenship examination.

I: But then it isn't a real democracy!

N: I would say it's a better democracy. Just look around the world. Everybody has the same right to vote everywhere, whether they understand political, economic, ecological or other issues or not, whether they are interested and concern themselves with them or not.
What's the point of the nonsense with the election placards and even with the electoral campaign? If the voters' behaviour is oriented towards it, it's no wonder all democracies are in crisis. Someone who isn't interested in politics and doesn't have a minimum of understanding for the background situation shouldn't vote. But it's no problem for someone who's interested to pass the citizenship examination and obtain the right to vote.

I: I hadn't looked at it from that point of view up to now.

N: Then you should. I can tell you that the time before elections is on quite a different level than it used to be. Now it's really about questions of content and not about someone's smile or another person's dirty laundry.

I: You don't have any parties?

N: No, parties are the death of democracy. Your Basic Law says that the members of parliament (MPs) are elected in a public, direct, free, equal and secret ballot and that they aren't bound by instructions. And what really happens? Half the MPs aren't directly elected but are delegated by the party whose list they are on. So you vote for a party and it chooses the MPs for you. And they are bound by the "party discipline." What else is that but instructions, I beg of you?

And so someone is elected in an election for a federal state parliament or a town council only because they're in the same party as the German Chancellor, whom the voter was more or less satisfied with, or vice versa. But the one person has nothing to do with the other.

No, nothing like that happens here. Every MP or councillor is elected personally and they're solely responsible to their consciences.

I: That's bound to produce quite different politicians, isn't it?

N: Certainly. A person's integrity is the most crucial thing for us. Nobody can hide behind some party decisions or suchlike.

I: Okay. On to my next question. At the council meeting there was a question about a retirement house. What's that?

N: That's a project of our pension system, German Pension. It builds retirement houses suitable for elderly people with several small rented units and a common area from the contributions the insured pay every month. As soon as somebody retires they get a flat in such a retirement house free of charge. That's virtually the pension they get plus a sum of money geared to their needs.

I: And if they already have a house?

N: Then the flat they're entitled to can be let to another person and they get the income from it. The system is fairly new. As soon as the first houses are ready, normal blocks of flats that can be let to families will be built, creating great flexibility.

I: And one day the whole country will be full of houses?

N: No, of course not. At some point there'll be enough houses and they'll last several generations with the sustainable building method used here. Then only the cost of maintaining them will be necessary and the contributions to German Pension will then be reduced accordingly. In that way it will be possible to realise a very inexpensive pension system with a high quality of life for elderly people within just a few years.

I: How did you actually manage to be debt-free in such a short time after the changeover?

i
p. 179

N: Oh, that was really easy.
After the changeover people started to change euros into Reichsmarks. Although they were rather hesitant at first, when every person had changed about 15% of their euros there were enough Reichsmarks in the Reichsbank to repay the entire debts of the town in one go – without anybody having to suffer losses. People had the same purchasing power after changing their money as before.

I: So the same thing would be equally possible in every community?

N: Absolutely. The percentage that would have to be changed differs of course. It depends on the community's debts and the population's savings, but the principle is equally applicable everywhere.
And since the changeover the town has had so many new and stable sources of income that there won't be any more debt problems in future.

I: Okay. I have just two more questions.

It seemed to me that you have only very few pharmacies. Is that correct?

N: That's an interesting question. It's quite possible. I only know that the sales of medicines have decreased enormously during the last few years. German Health's programmes have considerably enhanced the population's general health consciousness. Personal responsibility in health matters has grown greatly because of

that. That's why people increasingly use old proven home remedies and don't immediately go to the doctor or pharmacy for
everything.
I guess that the pharmacies we used to have weren't all able to
survive financially.

I: And my last question is about religion. I saw a synagogue and
       there was talk of a mosque. What is the state's attitude to those?

N: We have complete freedom to practise any religion as long as
       nobody is harmed by it. Each community can regulate the details
       itself. In the Kingdom we now have a community consisting al-
       most exclusively of Muslims. Religious freedom also prevails there
       in accordance with the Constitution but the people there have
       agreed to orient public life very strictly towards Islam. Why not?
       There are no specific regulations about that from the side of the
       state.

I: What happens at schools? Do they have religious instruction?

N: The general religious instruction at school is rather directed at
       ethics and broadening awareness, which is ultimately meaningful
       for any religion.
       In our PR work we at the Academy actually distance ourselves
       somewhat from the traditionally church-oriented religions and
       tend more towards a kind of universal religion. The reason for
       that is that with us natural science and religion increasingly over-
       lap because we also scientifically investigate fields previously re-
       served to religion or esotericism and, on the other hand, that
       we also integrate so-called paranormal phenomena into scientific
       explanatory models. This means that the divide between science
       and spirituality is disappearing in general but at the same time an
       increasingly concrete common core of all religions is emerging,
       so to speak the core of experience that one religion traditionally
       describes and names in one way and another in a different way.
       As soon as we realise that these are the same experiences, the
       traditional differences become less and less relevant and at the
       same time a greater and greater part of spirituality, which used
       to be dressed up as religion, belongs to the everyday horizon of
       experience.

I: That sounds interesting. But there are still church services and
       similar things all the same?

N: Yes, of course. Everyone is free to practise and believe what they like, also together with other like-minded people.

I: Norbert, thank you very much for taking so much time and trouble for me. But now it's really time for your family …

And, as if at a signal. Beatrice comes storming in and jumps on to her dad's lap.

B: Look at my lovely dress.

She positions herself again and circles gracefully to show off her dress.

N: Very nice. Did Mum give it to you?

B: Yes, we've prepared the things for the baby together.

I stand up and go up to Sabine.

I: I'd like to thank you so much for your hospitality. It was very interesting for me even if I completely disrupted your Sunday.

S: No problem. That's all right. I'm glad it was interesting for you. Norbert is still the best teacher. It's his calling and he just lives it.

Norbert takes me to the door. I ask him to explain briefly where I can find Dieter's firm and say a warm farewell.

On the way back to my hotel his final words "See you again soon!" sound in my ears for a long time like a promise.

Today's conversation has given me so many new impulses and shown me so many possibilities I hadn't previously even remotely thought of and at the same time raised so many more questions that I feel downright disoriented. What am I supposed to do with all this new experience? I can't just put it in a drawer like a souvenir from a trip.

A lot of conflicting thoughts whirl around in my head until I finally fall asleep.

My sleep is restless and probably not very refreshing either for when my alarm clock rings in the morning I feel totally knackered. In spite of that I jump up for my train goes at 8.50 am and I want to visit Dieter's firm before that.

So I hurriedly pack my things, have breakfast, pay and set off on my way to the address Norbert described to me. Somehow I must have overlooked something. At any rate I walk in a circle until I finally reach my destination a little late.

It's a strangely hectic morning and I feel so hounded as if someone is constantly pushing me to do something. I'm all the more astonished when I enter the firm. Here it's as if all the tension has stayed outside the door. Inside the premises there is a very pleasant atmosphere. I can't exactly say what the reason is.

D: Hallo, good morning.

I am greeted straightaway by Dieter, who has seen me from his office.

I: Good morning. Here I am.

D: That's good. Nice to see you.

I: You have a nice atmosphere here.

D: Yes, don't we? It strikes you immediately, doesn't it? We arranged everything according to Feng Shui principles. So everyone who works here is optimally supported. It's so important to feel good at work so that you can develop your full potential.

He shows me round the premises. They are furnished in varied ways, the lighting is agreeable and soft music is to be heard in the background.

Then he shows me the relaxation room, a darkened, sound-proofed room with a few mattresses on the floor.

D: This is our relaxation room. Everyone who is affected by a fit of fatigue is encouraged to come here and lie down for a few minutes.

I: Aha! During work time?

D: Whenever fatigue overcomes them. Fatigue doesn't always necessarily mean the need to sleep. It is often only a signal from the body that it needs a horizontal position for some metabolic processes. If it gets that, it is often fit again after a few minutes. But if it doesn't get it, you're tormented for ages.

I: I know that very well. Perhaps I should try it out, too.

D: Yes, it really works wonders. We used to go to the coffee machine to solve the problem. But now we use this way and have had good experience with it. The staff feel much better, are more alert and concentrated on their work and more productive on balance, even if they disappear into this room for ten minutes from time to time.

I: I assume that doesn't apply to sleeping in late after a night on the tiles?

D: Of course not. If necessary, we give a warning if someone uses this room conspicuously often or for a long time but that hardly ever happens.

I: So that's completely in line with the principle of trust again?

D: Exactly. The staff like to use the room in their lunch break as well to digest in peace and then go back to work refreshed.

I: How many people work here?

D: Four in production and two more in the office – a construction draftsman for the planning, a part-time employee for the commercial side and an apprentice.

I: Oh, you train people?

D: Yes, we do. State enterprises are encouraged to train apprentices and people who are retraining. Firms of a certain size are even obliged to do so. I like doing it because my job is fun for me and I like to pass something of it on to others.

I: And what is the training like with you?

D: Quite different from the old system.

I: Well, who would have thought that!

I reply with a laugh.

D: For instance, we don't have a vocational school. Actually that never really worked. The vocational school and the training firm also pursued different interests and that's why there wasn't any productive exchange.
    People have generally acquired the fundamental theory at school

and the nice thing is that they also really understood it there. They acquire everything else when they encounter it during their training.

I: All on their own without any help?

D: No. We are in a firm with other staff and the master craftsman. And if it gets really complicated at some point, the guild can help.

I: The guild?

D: Yes, we've revived the craft guilds as they used to be when the journeymen took to the road.

I: Didn't they travel around?

D: Exactly, but not just at their whim but from country to country, from building site to building site and from master to master. That had the critical advantage that they were able to get to know and try out many different kinds of work and working methods in the same profession. In that way new master craftsmen, who were better than their predecessors, emerged as they were able to combine the latter's knowledge in themselves and, in turn, passed it on.
Such a thing isn't possible with training in a single firm with only one teacher. The entire knowledge in all its diversity can't be passed on by a single individual.

I: And you've reintroduced the old system?

D: Yes, we have. It actually starts before the apprenticeship. For we strongly promote short-term and medium-term work internships. When the youngsters have finished their schooling, they go to various firms and do a work placement in each of them until they realise where their talents lie and what they would like to do. Their apprenticeship only starts after that.
There isn't any fixed time for the training. Everyone trains for either a short or a long time until they are finished. But it is compulsory to have trained in at least three firms, similar to taking to the road as the journeymen did.

I: Doesn't that make for huge confusion?

D: No, on the contrary it stimulates and keeps you alive. In this way the young people don't stay three years in one training firm and get bored to death but they get around, meet new people and get to know new working methods.

I: That sounds very interesting!

D: Shall we go over to production?

He takes me along a corridor to a storeroom and from there to a hall with several wood-working machines.

Here it is naturally much noisier than in the offices but it still does not feel like a usual factory floor. Is it the arrangement of the machines, the agreeable lighting or the refreshing coloured elements on the floor, ceiling and walls? I cannot make it out exactly but somehow the interaction of these factors generates a good feeling in me as if I were at home in my own workshop. The sequence of rooms fits together and the rooms have the appropriate connections. Everything is clean and tidy and in its proper place.

I observe the various stages of work and the interaction of the staff, starting with the machine room and a cleanroom and going on to the surface treatment and finishing with the assembly of the furniture. For training there is even a teaching workshop in a separate room.

Here it also becomes clear that the architecture of the whole building is geared to the production cycle. Together with the means of production and the interior fittings, economic, ecological and ergonomic concerns are combined in an impressive way. It really is a model firm.

We go back to the office area.

I: What are your working hours like?

D: Well, they're just changing – following the decision in the town council yesterday. We're now introducing a 30-hour working week!
      I still have to agree with the staff if they would rather work 5 days of 6 hours or 4 days of 7.5 hours.
      A middle way with a shorter Friday is also thinkable.

I: A 30-hour week! That's half my working time as a self-employed person!

D: Yes, I know!

We finish at 2 and then still have more than half the day in front of us!

I: What about the breaks?

D: We have an hour's lunch break. We introduced that relatively early on and all the staff are satisfied with it. At the beginning we tried doing without a lunch break and finished earlier but we all realised we feel better if we have a good lunch and then relax. Then we just have more from the rest of the day and it also has a very positive impact on our health. That's why nobody wants to go back to the old schedule.

I: And you can simply decide that for yourselves?

D: Of course, it's my firm after all. And we all sat down and decided on this solution together.

I: But isn't it a state enterprise?

D: Yes, but I'm the managing director.

I: Okay. And state enterprises don't pay tax, do they?

D: That's right, although private companies don't pay tax either.

I: Oh yes, except if they make harmful products.

D: Exactly. And I get a fixed salary here, which is convenient.

I: Don't you have to do any accounting then?

D: That isn't prescribed for private firms. But of course everyone does a simple revenue-expenditure surplus account to have an overview of the revenue and expenditure. On the other hand, it's compulsory for the state enterprises because the Reichsbank wants and has to get an overview of how business is going from time to time. The extent of the detail and breakdown of the account is actually decided by each firm itself.

I: And is auditing done?

D: It is in the state enterprises for there it's a question of the public weal and the state budget. A strict check must be kept on them as they have to earn surpluses. If that isn't the case, the reason is examined and ways to improve things are implemented. But auditing is done quite differently from what you outside are used to. Our goal is to help the entrepreneur and show them how they can do things better.

Private firms aren't audited for that's the private entrepreneur's own business. If someone goes bankrupt one day, that's their own problem. At any rate, the Reichsbank continually offers seminars for entrepreneurs to both types, so nobody is left out in the rain.

I: Wouldn't it have been an easier way to establish a private firm?

D: Yes and no. The accounting and auditing isn't the major issue. After all, every sensible business does that. But as a private firm I would have to bear all the investments myself: The whole building, the machinery, the store, the office, that's a lot of money. The state took over all the costs and I have been receiving my agreed salary from day one. Then there are the costs of the raw materials. As a private firm I would have had to purchase the wood whereas I get it free of charge as a state enterprise.

I: Why's that?

D: Because the Constitution says that all natural resources like land, minerals, water and wood are public property and thus part of the state assets.

I: Okay, I understand.

D: Of course I can't become infinitely rich with a state enterprise as the profits don't go into my pockets, but that isn't my goal at all. Here I have a very good salary and social insurance without any deductions from my pay and can still operate in a completely entrepreneurial way.

I: How does it work with investments? Is permission required every time?

D: No. I can operate freely with the business capital, Of course, if I would like to invest more than the money available, I have to talk to the Reichsbank. As a private firm, I would then have to take out a loan, whereas as a state enterprise I get the money from the Reichsbank but of course have to convince them that the investment makes sense and will pay off.

I: I must say that when I heard the word "state enterprise" I immediately had a bad aftertaste from the past.

D: Yes,

   Dieter laughs.

D: That's clear to me. But an enterprise doesn't have to be bad just
because it's a state enterprise! But, conversely, an enterprise
doesn't have to do well just because it's private. Additionally,
there's the matter of the frequently lacking responsibility for the
common good. You can see that in the situation in the FRG.
Since the German railway company Deutsche Bahn was privatised, there have been strikes, train cancellations, closure of lines,
higher fares, etc. That not only adversely impacts the economy
but the whole of society.
Or when Nokia simply decides to close their plant for economic
reasons and relocate to a cheaper country, they don't care in the
slightest that thousands of families lose their livelihood.

I: Yes, that's right. With us only economic interests count, and that
means profit.

D: That's how it is, unfortunately. That's why I think it's irresponsible to place the fate of the business in private hands above a certain size, number of employees or overall social importance of the
product or service. For, as a rule, the owners are only interested
in maximising profit and there is no possibility for the population
to exert an influence.
The private owners only think of their own interests, while here
matters of consequence to the whole of society are involved.
When such private firms make a profit, it goes into private pockets instead of into the state coffers. But when they're in difficulties, they call for help from the state coffers, as it involves a large
number of jobs, etc.
This was most blatant after the merger with the GDR. The former
state enterprises were privatised for next to nothing, often by
competitors from West Germany, who then simply closed down
profitable companies so as not to jeopardise their market position. Interests of common good played absolutely no part in these
transactions!

I: Something like that would probably not be possible in the King-dom, would it?

D: Here it would be a violation of the Constitution, which says that property involves an obligation and its use should simultaneously also serve the common good.

I: And who controls that?

D: The King as protector of the Constitution.

I: Okay, that's correct. I'd almost forgotten again that there's someone who ensures the Constitution isn't violated. I must say that's a wonderful thing.

D: It certainly is. I still know what it was like outside in the old sys-tem. Although you had all the nice provisions of the Basic Law and regulations in other laws as well, the authorities themselves didn't keep to them at all. They knew exactly that nobody would go to court for that. That's why they could be so unabashed.
I often thought: "If I had a legal costs insurance, I would sue them now." But then there's the whole trouble with a lawyer, court pro-ceedings and so on and so forth and at the end you don't know what secret agreements they come to. So nobody wants that and mostly has no time for it either.

I: And so they just continue with their arbitrariness.

D: Of course, but who has once gone to court in such a case?

I: Nobody, including myself. That's why the situation in the King-dom makes total sense to me.
But now I think I must be on my way. I have to go back to the old system. There I also have a firm and someone is just doing a tax audit on me. That's sheer horror.

D: Oh dear. Then I can only wish you lots of luck and stamina.

I: Thank you. I can well do with that.
But the weekend here has helped me gain greater self-confidence. If they keep on bugging me, I'll simply close my firm and move to the Kingdom.

D: That's a good idea! Anyone who takes an active stand for the common good is welcome here. I wish you a good trip.

I: Thank you. Good-bye and maybe see you again soon.

D: Yes, see you again soon.

He takes me to the exit and I rush to the station. There is very little time left but I am on the platform almost punctually at ten to nine. My train is already ready to leave but has to wait 10 minutes for a delayed connecting train. I get on, sit down by the window and first of all take a deep breath.

What a weekend that was! It was incredible what I had experienced and seen in those two days! I let my mind go over some points and experiences again.

But then I ask myself: What next? Should I now go home and just continue as previously? Is that possible at all? Shall I again place myself under the yoke of a state which is not a state at all and views and treats me as a member of its staff and now wants to milk me more than it has so far by means of a tax audit? Shall I continue to let myself be worn down by nerve-wracking bureaucracy, regulations hostile to life and senseless prohibitions until the enjoyment and fun I have in any activity has totally vanished?

Now that I have seen with my own eyes that things can be different with free people in a real state as partner and servant of its citizens, without an obligation to pay taxes, with the principle of trust, with an orientation towards people instead of an excessive flood of laws, regulations, decrees, guidelines and prohibitions.

Should I pack my suitcase and move to Talweis or another community in the Kingdom? That would make a lot of things easier and nicer for me. I could also inform people in our community about the new possibilities and work on our changing over to the Kingdom as well! But what would all my friends say? They would think I was completely crazy.

I could also first of all just continue as before and wait and see how everything develops. If I have had enough, I can still pack my suitcase. Now I know there is a train I can jump on at any time if there is a collapse. But isn't that unfair to all those who don't know anything about the Kingdom yet?

Somehow I must have nodded off during these conflicting thoughts. For after a while – I have no idea how long – I suddenly hear a voice calling: "Hallo, wake up! You must get off!"

What, get off already? I have only just got on!

As I am coming to myself, I feel someone shaking my shoulder and then I gradually wake up.

Norbert is standing in front of me. How come? And where am I? We are alone in a train.

N: Quick, the train is about to leave.

What train? I am totally confused. I pull myself together with an effort and follow Norbert who leads me out of the train on to the platform. But that is the train I arrived in! And there at the platform opposite another train is standing with the man and woman who were sitting opposite me on the outward journey at the door. They wave to us, we get on and at the same moment there is a whistle and the train starts moving.

We sit down on the nearest seats.

I am completely numbed, look around in surprise and see some faces I can remember from the outward journey.

Did I perhaps only dream everything?

That would be incredible! It was all so real ...

The shock still sits deep in my bones but gradually I come to myself again and no longer perceive my surroundings as dulled.

It is unimaginable! I believe I have discovered and experienced who knows what and also wonder if I should keep it to myself or pass it on to others. And now I fell asleep and nearly missed my train connection, which would have left me all on my own.

How glad I suddenly am to be with the others again although I do not actually know them. But at any rate we are going in the same direction together.

No, that has been enough in any case! I have understood the message for myself. Whatever has happened or is going to happen, I must not wait too long and must jump on the train in time. Otherwise it might leave without me! What was the saying: "Life punishes latecomers" or something like that?

I have often dreamt of things that have not yet happened. Is this another case? Or was it a pipedream?

The announcement on the loudspeaker jerks me out of my thoughts.

"Our next stop is Talweis. You will be in time for all your connections in spite of the delay."

Epilogue

Am I awake or dreaming?

That is what we often wonder if a situation is not as we were expecting it to be. Mostly we would prefer it not to be reality but a (bad) dream.

The focus should not be on this question here. Rather it should be clear to us that an idea we would like to be reality can at the same time be an impulse to act. When we have had an experience – even if it was "only" a dream – it is up to us to make it reality.

We should not underestimate the power of our thoughts and deeds but should use them and bundle them so that the negativity which is currently real can be forgotten like a bad dream and our best dreams can become reality instead.

Expression of thanks

My profound thanks go to

- Peter – for the vision, showing that it is legally feasible and the concrete impulses for implementing it,

- all those who have helped and are helping to build up what we have today,

- the many who will come to accomplish the vision,

- you personally for accepting and passing on the vision and letting it mature.

Thank you!

More in-depth information

Vaccinations

Vaccinations are considered one of the greatest medical achievements of the last 200 years. They are based on the theory that different diseases are caused by micro-organisms, against which the body can develop specific antibodies. When such antibodies are present in the blood, no disease occurs or at least the body can cope with it better. To stimulate the formation of such antibodies, the patient is given pathogens which are weak enough not to lead to disease but strong enough for antibodies to be formed against them.

To implement this in theory very plausible method large quantities of pathogens must first be cultivated. For bacteria this can be done relatively simply on growth media consisting of water, salts, sugar and amino-acids, whereas so-called viruses can only be reproduced in living cells. Depending on the pathogen, chicken tissue, monkey kidney cells, incubated chicken eggs (chicken embryos) and tissue from aborted human embryos are used for this.

To weaken their virulence, i.e. their pathogenic properties, the pathogens are deliberately bred in the tissue of foreign hosts, in which they are no longer virulent but can still reproduce. That is also partly achieved by breeding the pathogens at adverse low temperatures or adding formaldehyde. Other possibilities consist in using only fragments of pathogens or dead pathogens.

As practice has shown that the immune response provoked by pathogens obtained in this way is insufficient, they are enriched with so-called adjuvants, i.e. additives having the task of provoking a strong immune response. These are aluminium salts, primarily aluminium hydroxide and aluminium phosphate.

Finally, the vaccine is freed from any viruses that may still exist and preserved. This is done by adding formaldehyde and thiomersal (a mercury-containing compound).

The problems of the cocktails thus created are evident:
1. Even with most thorough cleaning it cannot be ruled out that the vaccine may still contain traces of foreign protein (from humans, chicken or monkeys), which may lead to strong allergic reactions in the vaccinated person.

2. The aluminium contained in the adjuvants is known for its toxic effects on the nerve tissue and is linked to Parkinson's disease, multiple sclerosis and dementia.

3. Formaldehyde is known to cause cancer and damage the liver and is therefore banned by law in the furniture industry, among others.

4. Thiomersal consists of 50% mercury and is known as a strong cell toxin and neurotoxin with allergenic and mutagenic impacts.

5. The question arises as to whether immunity against the actual pathogens is really achieved. At any rate, considerable changes were made to the pathogens and the actual immune response is not in fact provoked by the pathogens at all but by the additives.

The above-mentioned problems gain an especial significance particularly with vaccinations for new-born babies and infants. Due to their small body weight, even a single vaccination of a baby 25 times exceeds the limit for a risk-free intake of aluminium through infusions.

Furthermore, a child's immune system is not fully developed until it is one year old. Interventions in this phase can have repercussions for its entire later life, e.g. the development of allergies or auto-immune diseases (pathological overreactions of the immune system), on the one hand, or a weak immune system, on the other.

The nervous system also only develops during the course of the first few years of life. Thus, the so-called blood-brain barrier (a protective barrier between the central nervous system and the blood circulation) is still very permeable in infants so that the neurotoxins in vaccines can easily penetrate it. The protective myelin layer around the nerve cells also develops only gradually.

Babies that are breastfed, on the other hand, benefit from the mother's immune protection so that vaccination does not make sense anyway at that age.

Certain risks may of course be accepted if it means that dangerous infectious diseases in society will be repressed or even eradicated. The whole of vaccination has ultimately been based on this from the beginning. But unfortunately exactly this result – that vaccinations protect effectively against diseases – has not been scientifically proved up to today. So far, not a single comparative study of vaccinated and non-vaccinated people (double blind study) has been made to show that vaccinated people have a health advantage over non-vaccinated.

Therefore the success of a vaccination is determined today by measuring the antibody titre, i.e. the number of antibodies in the blood. Yet it is questionable whether this antibody titre says anything about the actual protection from disease, as in practice it is certainly possible to be immune even with a deficient titre and, on the other hand, to date no scientific study has been conducted to show that a high titre means protection from disease.

On a closer look, the numerous statistics showing how the importance of big epidemics has drastically declined over long periods of time (measured by the number of diseased or fatalities) simultaneously show that this decline had already started before vaccination started, that is was not positively but rather negatively influenced by large targeted vaccination campaigns, that it even continued unchanged after a (temporary) end to vaccination programmes and above all, that it affected all infectious diseases alike – whether a lot, a few or no people were vaccinated against them. Thus, these statistics show in reality that the actual causes of this decline were not vaccinations but greater hygiene, improved living conditions, eating habits and the social and technical standards of the last 200 years.

Climate warming

For some years much has been heard and read about climate warming and the so-called greenhouse effect. In particular CO_2 (carbon dioxide) is the focus as an infrared-active molecule, since its share in the atmosphere is influenced by combustion processes and thus partly also by human activity.

More than 150 years ago, it was found that different substances absorb different bands of the electromagnetic spectrum to varying degrees. Infra-red radiation is absorbed by molecules with a dipolar structure. In the atmosphere these are, above all, water and carbon dioxide as well as methane and laughing gas. Although a connection to Earth's climate was repeatedly investigated, it was ultimately dismissed as not relevant.

That suddenly changed in the 1960's and 1970's for a completely different reason. At that time, the first spacecraft were sent to Venus. It was assumed that the temperatures and pressure on its surface were similar to those on Earth. However, the first craft failed due to the high temperatures and pressure prevailing there. Venera 7 was the first spacecraft that managed to land. It was found that the surface temperature was over 450°C and that the atmosphere on Venus consists almost exclusively of carbon dioxide. This was not only a surprise but a shock for scientists. For as early as 1950 Immanuel Velikovsky, an outsider, had predicted just such surface conditions in his book *Worlds in Collision* [9]. These predictions originated from a detailed analysis of mythological records from all cultures and regions of Earth, from which it could be conclusively inferred that some 3,500 years ago there had been instability in the planetary system and several near-encounters with Earth and Venus. These near-encounters changed the rotation axes and velocities of the two planets, among other things, and led to far-reaching, disastrous changes on the surfaces of the planets. Something similar occurred in near-encounters between Venus, Earth and Mars some 2,800 years ago.

At that time, there was violent opposition by the scientific establishment to such theories and methods as they were in conflict with the dogma of uniformity, according to which from the beginning only small, scarcely perceptible changes had led to today's appearance of Earth and the solar system. Velikovsky's book was outlawed, its publisher boycotted and the author labelled as a crackpot – and now, as the Venus missions empirically confirmed his conclusions, an alternative explanation had to be quickly found. This was done by the American physicist Carl Sagan, who was for many years the head of the smear campaign against Velikovsky and his books, by claiming that the high temperature on Venus was connected to the high CO_2 concentration in the atmosphere and originated from a run-away greenhouse effect. He presented this theory at a symposium of the American Association for the Advancement of Science (AAAS) on the subject and thus the idea of a greenhouse effect from infra-red active gases was soon accepted in the scientific world, for the alternative would have been having to acknowledge Velikovsky to be right.

Ten years later this fabrication was then applied to Earth and exploited, above all, by groups with political, and later also economic interests.

Scientifically, the greenhouse effect had actually been refuted by experiments over 100 years ago. At that time Professor Wood of John Hopkins University in Baltimore, USA conducted several experiments to investigate the functioning of a greenhouse. His experiments were recently successfully replicated by Professor Nahle in Mexico [12]. In these experiments it was found that infra-red radiation plays virtually no part in the functioning of a greenhouse. The warming is solely due to the fact that the greenhouse roof stops warmth being carried away by convection. It was simultaneously shown by the experiment that the warmed surface of the earth only releases a very small part (8%) of its warmth through radiation and almost exclusively through convection.

This destroys the basis of the theory of the greenhouse effect for this assumes that 77% of the warmth is released through radiation (which is then radiated back to Earth through infrared-active molecules).

A very good synopsis of the various aspects of the greenhouse effect is to be found in a treatise by Klaus Ermecke [13].

This physical background has been presented by the physicist Professor Gerlich from the Technical University of Braunschweig [14]. Norbert's argumentation in the novel ("Checkmate in five moves") also originates from this presentation.

We will quote briefly from Gerlich's work here as it concisely summarises the crucial facts:

"It is an incontestable fact that the difficulties described here concerning the validity of all global climate models are known to the so-called "climatologists." When the "climatologists" took over from the politicians (IPPC) the task of using models to calculate climate changes ☞ caused by the change in the concentration of carbon dioxide, they p. 181 deliberately lied and deceived the public, as they knew exactly that numeric 'calculations' approximating to reality are never possible and never will be. ...

In addition, there is the modern practice of 'think-tanks' that undermine democratic decision-making processes because lay people or voters cannot criticise 'experts.' Such commissions (such as Hartz, PISA, IPCC, etc.) create expenses and always prove that they were important and necessary at the end of their work. They always find convincing reasons for their eternal existence. Nobody is personally responsible for the nonsense they produce. These commissions release the elected Members of Parliament from their duties to pass laws using their own brains and consciences. Instead, the politicians rely on 'expert opinions' of anonymous think-tanks, thus escaping having to take responsibility. The 'scientists' commissioned by the 'think-tanks' then deliver the politically desired 'results' embellished with allegedly 'calculated' uncertainties. This is the typical, unfree 'proposal science' which only owes its right to exist to its political mandate. Especially the UN and EU commissions thus generate the necessity of a totalitarian dictatorship throughout the entire world." [14]

Anyone who finds these statements one-sided or exaggerated can read [15] the over a thousand emails from a worldwide climate research centre in Britain, which were made public in 2009. This incident was called "Climategate" in allusion to the Watergate scandal under President Nixon, as the emails reveal how data were manipulated, deviating research results suppressed and critical scientists were bullied. The emails are arranged [16] in chronological order to make them easier to deal with. In a very illuminating detailed study two long-standing meteorologists have shown how temperature records are manipulated on a large scale [17].

So what is the whole topic actually about?

First it is about – mostly mediocre – scientists who can suddenly present their work in an important light and have secured almost unlimited funding from public institutions for themselves and their research teams for an unforeseeable time. It is about sectors of the economy which have found a welcome basis for price increases, marketing of useless products and services, climate certificates and suchlike.

And it is about globalisation. Because of the global fear it generates, global climate warming provides a perfect pretext for imposing regulations, provisions, surveillance measures and levies at an international level.

But ultimately it is about the fact that only 3,500 years ago Earth underwent one of the greatest global disasters in its history, when mountain ranges rose up, land and ocean formations altered and layers of ice were formed, which humanity today still believes to be millions of years old. This brings us back to Immanuel Velikovsky [9, 10, 11]. So as not to have to accept the truth of his findings the greenhouse effect was first of all invented and today it is also used to distract us from the fact that Earth has still not found its equilibrium after the disaster – just like us humans, who are still compulsively trying again and again and again to make the trauma of violence, destruction and suffering they experienced become reality using the most diverse of means.

Taxes

On the internet we can find a wealth of statistical data which permit instructive conclusions on closer examination.

The sources we have used are:

The Statistisches Bundesamt / Federal Statistical Office (www.destatis.de),

the Bund der Steuerzahler / Federation of Tax-payers (www.steuerzahler.de),

the Bundesbank / Federal Bank (www.bundesbank.de)

and also various statistics portals such as de.statista.com.

1. In 2013 the expenditure for interest payments in the national budgets amounted to 65.9 bn euros [18].

2. Tax revenues of the federal government, the governments of the federal states and the municipalities totalled 619.7 bn euros in 2013 [19].

3. 334.4 bn euros were paid from the national budgets in debt repayments in 2013 [18].

4. Total expenditure of national budgets amounted to 1.2 bn euros in 2013 [18].

5. Interest earned by German financial institutions amounted to 220.8 bn euros in 2013 [20].

6. Interest payable by German companies amounted to 60.5 bn euros in 2013 [21].

7. Corporation tax paid by German enterprises amounted to 66.5 bn euros in 2013 [21].

8. Taxes on the income and profits of German enterprises amounted to 46.5 bn euros in 2013 [21].

9. External financing of German enterprises was reduced by 15.5 bn euros in 2013 [21].

10. Turnover of German enterprises totalled 5733 bn euros in 2013 [21].

11. Annual profit of German enterprises totalled 181.5 bn euros in 2013 [21].

12. Payroll expenses of German enterprises amounted to 894 bn euros in 2013 [21].

13. The advantage due to the reduced tax rate totalled 24.2 bn euros in 2008 [22].

14. Revenues from sales tax and import sales tax in the total national budget amounted to approx. 172 bn euros in 2008 [23].

15. The average rate of income tax in Germany was 19.6% in 2010 [24].

16. The rate of contribution to social insurance – apart from special regulations, excluding accident insurance and including insolvency bonus – was 39.6% as a rule in 2013 [25].

From 1. and 2. it can be concluded that on average 10.6% of the tax revenues was used for interest payments.

It can likewise be concluded from 2. and 3. that on average 54% of the tax revenues was used for debt repayments.

This already makes 64.6% going directly to the banks.

What happens to the rest of the tax revenues (35.4%)? They are spent as investments, salaries, grants, subsidies, social benefits, etc. Overall, it can be said that they go back into economic circulation – directly or indirectly. For the sake of simplicity, we must assume for the calculation that the money remains in Germany and we have to ignore taxes on wages and supplementary wage costs, which immediately land in the public budget again – albeit only in the case of ordinary employees but not with civil servants.

Under these conditions the money is thus paid to a German company at some time or other in order to purchase a product or service- However, value-added tax has to be paid on this amount at a rate of either 19% or 7%.

Points 13. und 14. indicate that in 2008 goods and services worth some 829 bn euros were subject to 19% tax and goods and services worth some 208 bn euros to 7% tax. Thus, the mean rate of value-added tax was 16.6% for that year. This mean rate of value-added tax is also the basis for our calculation for 2013.

Hence, 35.4% of the tax revenues was used to purchase goods and services with an average rate of value-added tax of 16.6%. The value-added tax revenues thus obtained were, again, used for interest payments (10.6%) and debt repayment (54%) (see above).

The enterprise's net sales remain after deduction of value-added tax.

According to 7., 8. and 10. the share of the corporation and profits taxes of German enterprises amounted to some 2% of their total turnover in 2013.

Thus 2% of the turnover earned above went back to the government as taxes, which, again, were used for interest payments (10.6%) and debt repayment (54%).

According to 6., 9. and 10. expenditure by German enterprises for interest payments and repayment of external debt amounted to some 1.3% of the total turnover. Thus, 1.3% of the turnover earned above went to the banks.

10., 11. and 12. reveal that in 2013 on average 18.8% of the turnover of German enterprises consisted of wages, salaries and profit for the owners/shareholders.

Assuming that the average rate of income tax did not change much from 2010 to 2013, according to 15. on average 19.6% of this went to the government budget as income tax and according to 16. some 39.6% as social insurance, and, again, this amount was used for interest payments (10.6%) and debt repayment (54%).

77.9% of the turnover remains to be used for other expenses and thus finally for purchasing goods and services from other enterprises. As value-added tax is only a transitory item in business between enterprises, this 77.9% thus constitutes direct turnover of other enterprises, with which we have to proceed and calculate as before.

If everything is added up and we approximate the sum which potentially stretches into infinity by the summation formula for geometric series, there is a total of 81.9% of tax revenues which end up in the banks directly or indirectly as interest payments and debt repayment.

In other words, if there was to be a total cancellation of interest payments and debt repayments today, tomorrow only 18.1% of today's taxes would have to be paid so as to make the same financial resources available to the community as today.

Creation of money

The process of money creation by the central banks is certainly easily comprehensible and logical.

But we would like to explain the process of creating deposit money with a concrete example borrowed from Bernd Senf [26]:

Let us assume that customer A pays 100 euros in cash into his current account at his bank. His bank credits the 100 euros to his account. This deposit is known as a demand deposit. The customer can make use of the money at any time by means of a cashless transfer or a cash withdrawal.

Now, the bank does not just leave the 100 euros lying around until the customer perhaps withdraws some of it one day. If the customer transfers money to another customer B of the same bank, the bank does not even need to touch the 100 euros, as it only needs to debit an amount from A's account and pay it into B's account on the computer. The bank thus has certain experience as to what percentage of its deposits is necessary in cash reserves (minimum reserves in banking terminology) in order to be able to cope well with the ongoing withdrawals and transfers to other banks. In addition, there are the statutorily prescribed minimum reserves it has to deposit with the central bank. The bank wants to work with the rest of the money.

What figures are we talking about here? The bank reserves amount to some 3% of the demand deposits in total, so that the bank will work with 97%. That means it will keep only 3 of the 100 euros paid in as reserves. 97 euros are surplus reserves, concerning which it has incidentally not even been clarified by law whom they belong to. Since this has not been clarified by law, the bank considers it to be in order to make use of the surplus reserves without informing customer A.

Now it might lend the 97 euros to another customer or it might act as if the 97 euros are the minimum reserves for a new loan. In this way it gives customer C a loan of 3233.33 euros, crediting the amount to C's account. For this demand deposit it has to show proof of 3% reserves, which is exactly the 97 euros it has still got from A.

The balance thus shows a liability of 3233.33 euros, since C may wish to make use of the amount of his loan. At the same time, it has a receivable due from C amounting to 3233.33 euros, as C has to repay this amount (plus interest and compound interest). The bank's balance thus shows 3233.33 euros both on the assets and the liabilities side – resulting in neither a profit nor a loss. However, the bank will earn interest on the 3233.33 euros or, if the customer is not able to repay the loan, it will absolutely legally take away the property he has used as collateral for the loan.

What has now in fact happened? The bank received 100 euros in cash and then gave a loan of 3233.33 euros – with pure booking procedures. In this way 3133.33 euros which were not there before at all have been "created." Although it is not cash, this deposit money can be used in an equally real way as cash can be.

Incidentally, this deposit money disappears again to the extent that customer C repays his loan.

Let us now consider the whole procedure from a completely different point of view.

The bank has carried out a few transfers, which have created money that customer C has to repay with interest, without the bank having to have done anything in return.

Let us compare that with the text of Section 291 of the German Criminal Code (StGB) on Usury:

(1) Whosoever exploits the predicament, lack of experience, lack of judgment or substantial weakness of will of another by allowing material benefits to be promised or granted to himself or a third person

1. for the rent of living space or additional services connected therewith;

2. for the granting of credit;

3. for any other service; or

4. for the procurement of one of the previously indicated services, which are in striking disproportion to the value of the service or its procurement, shall be liable to imprisonment not exceeding three years or a fine. If more than one person contribute as providers of benefits, procurers or in other ways, and if the result is thereby a striking disproportion between the sum of the material benefits and the value of the services, the 1st sentence above shall apply to each of the persons who exploits the predicament or other weakness of the other for himself or a third person in order to obtain excessive material benefits.

(2) In especially serious cases the penalty shall be imprisonment from six months to ten years. An especially serious case typically occurs if the offender
1. by the offence places the other in financial hardship;
2. commits the offence on a commercial basis;
3. accepts promissory notes representing usurious material benefit.

The bank is doing this very thing, as we have seen above – on a commercial basis.

Federal Reserve Bank

The Federal Reserve Bank (Fed) was established on 23.12.1913 by the Federal Reserve Act. This legislative procedure had been prepared and staged long before. As early as 1910, there was a secret meeting of some of the most influential bankers, who agreed to establish a private banking cartel, which was to be given the monopoly for issuing the US dollar by legislation. For this the President also had to be replaced as well as a great deal of lobbying work done. For this purpose, a new party, the Progressive Party, was founded in 1912; it was dissolved again in 1916 but it had a decisive influence on the outcome of the election in 1912. Only a few months after the new President Woodrow Wilson came into office, the vote on the law was scheduled for the day before Christmas, when only a small number of Members of Congress were expected to be present and attentive.

More details and background information can be found in the relevant literature [27, 3].

Fundaments of monetary law

In connection with money, one repeatedly encounters various terms which are mostly viewed as synonyms and are also used as such.

However, a closer look shows that these terms have greatly different meanings and, at the same time, are linked to a strictly defined legal background. Therefore we will take a closer look at them here.

First of all, money is a means of payment, for we want to buy and pay for goods and services with it. However, there is the distinction between public means of payment and legal means of payment. Besides that, there is the term currency or legal currency. What do all these terms mean?

1. Public means of payment
A public means of payment is a means of payment generally accepted in a specific area or society. That means that everyone has explicitly or tacitly agreed to accept this means of payment as such.

2. Legal means of payment
Unlike with public means of payment, there is a legal foundation for a legal means of payment. That means that a legitimate legislator has made the means of payment into a legal means of payment through a law. Therefore there is a compulsion to accept it and a statutory regulation regarding the making and distribution of counterfeit money.

3. Currency
The word "Währung [currency] " comes from Middle High German and has something to do with a guarantee (warranty). A currency is a means of payment that is linked to the right to something defined something equivalent in return. Thus, a currency can only exist when a legal foundation exists, i.e. it can only exist as a statutory currency.

4. Statutory currency
A statutory currency is a legal means of payment that was created on the basis of a law in a state and for which a permanent right to an equivalent in return for the previously rendered service is granted and guaranteed by law.

Thus, a currency also fulfils another function for which money is generally used: it is a means of conserving value.

For this it is essential that the money keeps its value, i.e. that for a specific amount of money you can obtain the equivalent in return to what you had to do to obtain the money – regardless of the time that has elapsed.

Money is thus an entitlement to consume in this case. When someone has rendered a service, they obtain a receipt in the form of a bank note guaranteeing their right to an adequate compensation. The state or the public corporation as the authority legitimized by and servant of the citizens is obliged by the law created to grant and guarantee this right to consume. Hence, the bank note is a document granting the right to claim adequate compensation for services previously rendered.

At the same time, the citizen has the obligation to accept this means of payment.

Let us consider some examples.

- The dollar is a legal means of payment through a law passed by the US Congress. However, the dollar is not a currency as it is issued by the Fed and lent at interest. Neither the Fed as a private bank nor the government, which is not the issuer of the dollar, can give a guarantee for the permanent value of the dollar. Thus dollar bills are not bank notes but only money bills.

i
p. 155

- In Germany the euro is only a public means of payment. Since the EU is neither a state nor a public corporation, the basis is lacking for a legal means of payment. Reference to the law about the Deutsche Bundesbank [German central bank] in the Federal Republic of Germany does not change anything about this fact since the Federal Republic of Germany is likewise not a state. There is no compulsion to accept it, such as belongs to a legal means of payment, as we can notice everywhere with the 500-euro notes.

i
p. 169

Likewise there is no right to consume or receive something in return anymore, which is the reason that the euro is not a currency. The high rate of price increases is further proof of this. The euro notes are thus not bank notes either and counterfeiters are only prosecuted for violation of copyright (see © symbol on the front, to the right of the European flag or in the bottom left corner).

- The mark (Goldmark) of the German Kaiserreich after1871 was a statutory currency. It was backed by gold, which was expressed by the text printed on the bank notes: "One hundred marks will be paid by the Reichbank's central pay office to the person presenting this bank note." In this way, adequate compensation was guaranteed. Counterfeiting was punished by law as a criminal offence. Therefore the bank notes bore the sentence: "Anyone who copies or counterfeits bank notes or obtains copied or counterfeit notes and circulates them will be sentenced to not less than two years imprisonment."

What are then the concrete, practical consequences of the type of money?

	Public/legal means of payment	**Statutory currency**
Prices	high inflation/ rate of price increases	price stability
Unemployment	high	none or low
Market behaviour	fierce competition, monopolies	fair
Bankruptcies	many	few
Poverty	widespread, increasing	little
Taxes and charges	high	none or few
Crime rate	high	low
Social structure	redistribution from poor to rich	equal chances for all
Exploitation of people and nature	great	small
Environment	destruction	conservation
	wars	peace

Due to the exponential growth pressure, a monetary system based on interest inevitably leads to fierce competition with ruthless striving for profit (by exploiting people and nature, destruction of the environment, crime, wars), a high inflation rate with increasing poverty, bankruptcies, monopolies and high unemployment.

When the purchasing power of the euro becomes lower and lower and the euro notes have less and less value (or one day none at all), it is not possible to take legal action; for nobody has given a guarantee as would be the case with a statutory currency.

Summary:

Requirements for a statutory currency:

1. A real state (with a people, state territory, state constitution and authorities legitimized by the people who can enact laws with legal effect).

2. The possibility for the state to create, print and issue money itself.

3. A law enacted by this state on which the legality of the currency is based.

4. Absence of interest and compound interest so as to be able to guarantee permanent stability of the value of the currency and guarantee every possessor of a means of payment the equivalent value in return for the service previously rendered even in future.

5. Backing of the paper money by values to permanently guarantee every holder of means of payment the right to consume.

State

In 1900 the German expert on constitutional law Georg Jellinek established a definition of a state, which he published as the "three-element theory" in his main work "Allgemeine Staatslehre [General theory of state]" [28]. According to this, a state is a social entity with the following three characteristics:

- state territory
- people
- authority

Since then this has been generally – also internationally – recognised as a definition and has become part of customary international law.

It is also to be found in the "Montevideo Convention on Rights and Duties of States" of 1933 [29], whose Article 1 defines a state as a person under international law, possessing Jellinek's three elements and the additional ability to establish a relationship to other states. Article 3 incidentally says that the existence of a state does not depend on its recognition by other states.

There are differing interpretations as to whether the Montevideo Convention is to be applied in general or only with respect to its signatories. However, in general it is interpreted as being valid for all subjects of international law, as it only codifies existing legal norms.

In Europe the common definition of a state is expressed in the first report of the Badinter Commission [30], which was established by the European Community on 27.7.1991 to make reports concerning international law against the background of the collapse of Yugoslavia and whose members were, among others, the then presidents of the German, French, Italian, Spanish and Belgian Constitutional Courts. In this report a state is defined as a community which consists of a state territory and a people which is subject to an organised political authority – which are again Jellinek's three elements.

Principle of subsidiarity

Subsidiarity (from Latin subsidium = help, reserve) is a legal and state concept, which – unlike the centralistic "Roman" state system – focuses on the individual and their self-realisation.

It says that an individual should be left to do what they are able to, and likewise a family, a larger group or a community of people must not be deprived of what they are able to accomplish themselves.

In general, it can be said that tasks, acts and solutions to problems should be undertaken as far as possible by the smallest group or on the lowest level of a form of organisation. Only when this is not possible or involves considerable hurdles and problems or the greater value of cooperation is obvious and generally agreed should successively larger groups, public collectives or higher levels of an organisation intervene in a subsidiary, i.e. supportive manner (source: Wikipedia, last accessed on 20.8.2015).

The principle of subsidiarity is orientated towards tribes as larger family structures, such as the customary Germanic tribes. These tribes were integrated into village communities, were connected to each other and gave each other mutual help and assistance.

After the reformation this principle found its way into the Calvinist conception of the community and in the 19th century into Catholic social doctrine as well.

Today the principle of subsidiarity is a principle to be applied in Germany pursuant to Art. 23 of the Grundgesetz [Basic Law] and in the EU pursuant to Art. 5 of the EU Treaty of Lisbon. Although it is not expressly mentioned, it is to be found from the start in Articles 1 and 2 (individual), 6 (family), 9 (mergers of larger interest groups) and 28 (communities as local corporations with legislative powers) of the Grundgesetz [Basic Law]

It is important that the benefit of the larger community making use of superordinate rights or reserving the right to make regulations as opposed to the smaller community or the individual has to be proved by the larger community in each case.

Furthermore, the larger community must withdraw again and wait for a possible fresh request for help when the smaller community's competence has grown through the aid given so that it can help itself to the extent that it can carry out these tasks at least in a comparable manner and desires to be independent of the larger community.

Here are two quotations from Otfried Höffe [32], professor of philosophy:

"On the other hand, the principle of subsidiarity reminds us that political power does not come from above and may be passed down as grace is. It is conferred from below by the civitas and is only transferred to the state on condition that it serves the civitas."

"In relation to the constituent states (federal states, départements or cantons), communities have, on the one hand, the right to manage their affairs themselves and, on the other hand, the right always to avail themselves of help when they are not able to cope with their tasks on their own."

Grundgesetz [Basic Law]

The Grundgesetz [Basic Law] constitutes the fundamental order of the Federal Republic of Germany; however, it is not a constitution. For there is always a vote (referendum) on a constitution. Through a referendum the people agrees to the drafting of a written fundamental order and accepts this as a general law due to its free voting decision. Only through this act does the constitution become binding law and come into existence as a "constitution". A free voting decision of the people is always required first for a fundamental order to become a genuine constitution.

This fact is confirmed by the Grundgesetz [Basic Law] itself:

Art. 146
This Basic Law, which since the achievement of the unity and freedom of Germany applies to the entire German people, shall cease to apply on the day on which a constitution freely adopted by the German people takes effect.

Appendix Unification Treaty
Art. 5
The governments of both parties recommend to the legislative authorities of the unified Germany to deal with the questions raised in connection with German reunification with respect to changing or amending the Basic Law within 2 years, particularly with the question of applying Art. 146 of the Basic Law and in this respect with a referendum.

Other articles cited in this book:

Art. 23
(1) With a view to establishing a united Europe, the Federal Republic of Germany shall participate in the development of the European Union that is committed to democratic, social and federal principles, to the rule of law, and to the principle of subsidiarity, and that guarantees a level of protection of basic rights essentially comparable to that afforded by this Basic Law.

(1a) The Bundestag and the Bundesrat shall have the right to bring an action before the Court of Justice of the European Union to challenge a legislative act of the European Union for infringing the principle of subsidiarity.

Art. 25
The general rules of international law shall be an integral part of federal law. They shall take precedence over the laws and directly create rights and duties for the inhabitants of the federal territory.

Art. 28
Municipalities must be guaranteed the right to regulate all local affairs on their own responsibility, within the limits prescribed by the laws.

Art. 133
The Federation shall succeed to the rights and duties of the Administration of the Combined Economic Area.

Constitutional principles

Constitutional principles are the fundamental principles of a democratic state. They are explicitly laid down in Section 92(2) of the Criminal Code [StGB]:

Section 92 of the Criminal Code [StGB]
(2) Constitutional principles, within the meaning of this law, shall be

1. the right of the people to exercise state authority in elections and ballots and through particular organs of legislative, executive and judicial power and to elect their representatives in general, direct, free, equal and secret elections;
2. the subjection of legislation to the constitutional order and the subjection of the executive and judicial power to law and justice;
3. the right to form and exercise a parliamentary opposition;
4. the replaceability of the government and its responsibility to the representatives of the people;
5. the independence of the courts; and
6. the exclusion of any government by force and arbitrary rule.

Conclusions:
The Lord Mayors and the directly elected councillors are the only ones who are elected in the way described above. They are thus the only representatives of the people. Neither the members of the Bundestag (lower house of the German parliament) nor the members of the Landtag (federal state parliaments) are elected in the samea direct and equal way. This was criticised by the German Constitutional Court in its decision 2 BvF 3/11 of 26 July 2012. Hence, they cannot and should not be representatives of the people.

With their representatives elected in the communities, the citizens of the towns and communities have the right to elect and exercise their state authority through special legislative, executive and jurisdictive organs (1st constitutional principle).

The towns and communities also have the right to subject themselves to a constitutional system and subject their legislation to this constitution (2nd constitutional principle). In this regard, the executive and the legislative in the community or town also have to adhere to this constitution and the subordinate laws.

The German people has the right to a parliamentary opposition. That does not mean that it requires a party in parliament to this end (3rd constitutional principle).

Every town and every community has the right to detach itself from the so-called "Bundesregierung [federal government]" and the "Landesregierung [government of the federal state]" (4th constitutional principle). It thus has the right to be fully autonomous or also to join another German government which as an opposition can exercise state authority.

Sovereignty of Germany

With regard to the question of Germany's status under international law, there are various levels of presenting and viewing it.

As we all know, Germany was occupied by the allied powers after the unconditional capitulation of the Wehrmacht (German armed forces) on 8.5.1945.

On 23.5.1949 the Bundesrepublik Deutschland [Federal Republic of Germany] was established on the territory of the three Western-occupied zones under the control of the occupying powers with the Grundgesetz [Basic Law] as constitution. The German Democratic Republic (GDR) was established with its own constitution on the territory of the Soviet-occupied zone on 7.10.1949.

On 5.5.1955 the Paris Peace Treaties, including the General Treaty (Germany Treaty) revoking the occupation statute of the Federal Republic of Germany, came into force [34].

With German reunification and the coming into force of the Two Plus Four Treaty as peace treaty on 15.3.1991 [35] Germany regained its full sovereignty as a state.

That is the superficial view of things as is taught in schools. If we take a closer look, we notice some peculiarities:

- Art. 1 (1) of the Paris Treaties or the Germany Treaty contained in them [34] states that the Federal Republic of Germany has "full power over its internal and external affairs." However, Art. 2 (1) says that "the Three Powers ... retain the rights they have hitherto exercised or held regarding ... Berlin and Germany as a whole."

- Furthermore, Art. 1 (2) states that the Allied High Commission will be dissolved. 35 years later, however, Article 1 of the Agreement Regulating Certain Issues Regarding Berlin of 25.9.1990 still speaks of the Controlling Council and the Allied High Commission.

- In Art. 5 of the Paris Treaties an important restriction was made on the sovereignty of Germany, namely for a case of emergency. For this reason, among others, the controversial emergency laws were passed on 30.5.1968. Thereupon, the Foreign Office announced on 31.5.1968 that the allies' rights to make reservations had now been revoked for good [37]. The following sentence is interesting: "The decisive difference ... is that the allies will no longer be active on account of the occupying rights reserved to them but German authorities on account of the German legislation binding on them." In other words, nothing changed; the occupying law was simply converted into German law.

Nevertheless the fact that further allied rights to make reservations still existed emerges from a declaration in the Bundesgesetzblatt [Federal Law Gazette] of 1990 [38].

The question arises as to how many such reservation rights still exist today.

- As part of the Paris Treaties the "Agreement on the rights and duties of foreign armed forces and their members in the Federal Republic of Germany" [39] was concluded. Furthermore, Germany joined NATO in 1955 and in 1959 concluded the "Additional agreement to the treaty between the parties to the North Atlantic Treaty on the legal status of their troops regarding the foreign troops stationed in the Federal Republic of Germany" [40]. Art. 3 lays down the obligation of the German authorities to cooperate closely with the troop authorities.

Thus, the impression cannot be dismissed that the rights of the occupying powers were (partly) revoked in the one agreement but newly concluded in other agreements, which incidentally still continue to be valid today even after reunification. The legal phrase "continued compliance with allied occupation rights by the Federal Republic of Germany" has become common usage.

- Art. 7 of the Two Plus Four Treaty of 12.9.1990 [35] states that the four allied powers terminate "their rights and responsibilities with regard to Berlin and Germany as a whole" and that "unified Germany … accordingly has full sovereignty over its internal and external affairs." However, in the days that followed there was an intensive diplomatic exchange of notes between Germany and the three allied powers concerning the Germany Treaty and the Transition Treaty and with other members of NATO concerning the Residence Agreement, the NATO Status of Forces Agreement and the Additional Agreement of 1959 [41, 42, 43, 44]. These notes agreed that NATO agreements were to remain in force and the Germany Treaty was to be suspended, but parts of the Transition Treaty [46] were to remain valid, including Art. 2(1): "All rights and obligations based on or determined by legislative, judicial or administrative measures by the occupying authorities or on the grounds of such measures are and remain in force under German law in every respect, regardless whether they are based on or determined in conformity with other legal provisions. These rights and obligations are subject without discrimination to the same future legislative, judicial and administrative measures as such rights and obligations based on or determined by domestic German law." That appears to be an exemplary model of carte blanche and is commented on in [45] in the following words: "On account of its declaratory character this exchange of notes does not require the consent of the legislative bodies and is not affected by German unity or the suspension of the rights and responsibilities of the Four Powers."

- In an extremely enlightening essay [47] the former German minister Egon Bahr describes how Willy Brandt had to confirm rights to make reservations, which all his predecessors in office had already confirmed, in three letters to the ambassadors of the three Western allies after being appointed Chancellor. How many such secret side-agreements still exist today?

Now we want to examine the matter again with regard to international law.

In the Berlin Declaration of 5.6.1945 [48] the allied powers stated that they would assume the supreme governing authority within the territory of the German Reich, having been granted the right to this through the unconditional capitulation of the German Wehrmacht (armed forces). This declaration emphasises that the assumption of governing power does not signify the annexation of Germany and moreover the "borders according to the status of 31 December 1937" were fixed as the basis for the organisation of the occupation.

Pursuant to Article 43 of the Hague Convention Respecting the Rules of War on Land, the occupying powers now were obliged "to undertake all measures to restore and maintain public order and public life as far as possible, observing national laws as far as no compelling obstacle existed."

For this purpose the united economic area was first of all created, initially consisting of the bizone (American- and British-occupied zones) and then expanded into the trizone including the French-occupied zone. At the same time, the three allied occupying powers set about establishing a new "West German" state. On 1.7.1948 they handed over to the prime ministers of the West German Länder the "Frankfurt Documents," [50] in which they laid down that a constituent assembly would be convened to elaborate a democratic constitution. After authorisation from the military governors this constitution was to be ratified by a referendum in the federal states. Furthermore, they stated how the occupying powers were to control the future German government.

Then the prime ministers of the Western zones met in Hotel Rittersturz near Koblenz and decided to accept these proposals only to a limited extent. They did not want the state of Germany to be divided and therefore agreed not to establish a proper state but only a temporary arrangement and accordingly not to elaborate a proper constitution either but only a "Grundgesetz [Basic Law]." These Koblenz Resolutions were published on 10.7.1948. Carlo Schmid, one of the fathers of the Grundgesetz [Basic Law] made the pregnant statement that "a state presupposes a people and there is no West German but only a German people." On 23.5.1949 the Grundgesetz [Basic Law] approved by the military governors of the three Western occupied zones and accepted by the "representatives of the people" of the federal states (without a referendum) was thus proclaimed and the "Bundesrepublik Deutschland [Federal Republic of Germany]," which pursuant to Art. 133 of the Basic Law took over "administration of the united economic area," was established. Shortly before, on 12.5.1949, the Occupation Statute of Germany was proclaimed by the three military governors and supreme commanders.

The procedure was similar in the Soviet-occupied zone with the GDR being established as the administrative construct.

Thus three legal entities then existed in Germany:

- The German Reich with the Weimar Constitution, which was occupied by the allied powers and unable to function because of the lack of institutions and office-holders. Regarding the constitution and laws, the status of 4.3.1933 is to be assumed, since the composition of the Reichstag (lower house of parliament) was unconstitutional following the elections of 5.3.1933 and hence no effective laws could be passed between 5.3.1933 and 8.5.1945. This was decided on 6.1.1947 by the Tribunal Général established by the allies in Rastatt.

- The Federal Republic of Germany (FRG) as a state-equivalent administrative construct of the three Western allied powers in the western occupied zones with the constitution-equivalent Basic Law as the fundamental order.

- The German Democratic Republic (GDR) as state-equivalent administrative construct of the Soviet Union in the Soviet-occupied zone with the GDR Constitution as the fundamental order (which did not become a proper constitution until after a referendum held in 1968).

On 31.8.1990, the FRG and the GDR concluded the Unification Treaty ("Treaty between the Federal Republic of Germany and the German Democratic Republic on the Establishment of German Unity") [52], which regulated the modalities of the unification of these two administrative constructs.

For this five new federal states were established on the territory of the GDR by the Ländereinführungsgesetz [Introductory Act on Federal States] on 22.7.1990. These states acceded to the FRG on 3.10.1990 after the GDR had dissolved itself on 2.10.1990.

Prior to this, the strange Two Plus Four Treaty [35] was concluded on 12.9.1990. The concluding parties were named as the four allied powers, the FRG and the GDR. However, almost the entire agreement then talks about "united Germany" – as an entity yet to be more precisely defined or created, which did not yet exist at all. Thus, Art. 9, for instance, states: "This agreement enters into force for united Germany, the French Republic, the United Kingdom of Great Britain and Northern Ireland, the Union of Socialist Soviet Republics and the United States of America on the day the last document of ratification or adoption is deposited by these states." According to this, "united Germany" is to be a state which is supposed to ratify this agreement. However, it was not listed as one of the parties to the agreement and neither was it precisely defined anywhere.

Art. 10 then states: "The original text of this agreement, whose German, English, French and Russian versions are equally binding, will be deposited with the government of the Federal Republic of Germany, which will provide the governments of the other parties to the agreement with certified copies." According to this, "united Germany" is obviously something different from the "Federal Republic of Germany" and so this agreement did not come into force at all according to Art 9 as only the Federal Republic of Germany ratified it but "united Germany" did not.

From a legal point of view the Two Plus Four Treaty is not a peace treaty, although it is always presented as such. That is already shown by its strange name "Treaty on the Final Settlement with Respect to Germany." A peace treaty can only be concluded between the parties waging war. but that was the German Reich on the German side.

A peace treaty would create clarity and provide binding answers under international law to the questions as to whether the German Reich should continue to exist and – if not – what is to be its legal successor. It would end the state of war and occupation effectively and for good. It would then also have to clarify what is all about and what is to be done with the occupying powers' administrative construct – the FRG. At the same time it would have to clarify what is to be done with the entire territory of the German Reich with its borders as of 31.12.1937, including the territories which are today under Polish or Russian administration.

And this seems to be the very reason why such a peace treaty does not yet exist, although peace treaties were concluded with Italy, Finland, Hungary, Rumania and Bulgaria already in 1947 and an inter-state treaty with Austria in 1955. As can be seen from the minutes of the third meeting of the Foreign Ministers of the Two Plus Four with intermittent participation of Poland on 17.7.1990 [53] in Paris, the Polish Foreign Minister addressed the issue of the guarantee for the western border of Poland there. Pursuant to Art. 7 of the Germany Treaty of 1955 [34], the definitive determination of Germany's borders will be postponed until there is a regulation through a peace treaty. Thereupon he was assured by Foreign Minister Genscher and it was noted in the minutes that these circumstances would not occur, i.e. a peace treaty or a regulation through a peace treaty are not planned.

In summary, it can be stated that an unclear situation prevails in Germany with respect to international law and politics. The German Reich still exists with its borders as of 1937 but it is incapable of acting, which is also confirmed by the jurisdiction of the so-called Constitutional Court (BVerfGE 36,1 III.1). Alongside this there is the FRG as the administrative construct established by the Western allied powers, which still does not possess any sovereignty because of the special regulations of the allied powers and about whose basic principles the population of Germany has never been democratically asked.

The governing powers obviously have no interest in clarifying this situation through a peace treaty. It will probably be endeavoured to maintain the present situation so long until it is established as common law.

In this way it is possible that existing secret agreements may also be "cured" as they otherwise could not be invoked as per Article 102 of the Charter of the United Nations. In this connection, we can also ask why the enemy state clause is still to be found in the United Nations Charter (Article 53, 107), stating that sanctions can be undertaken against a state which was an enemy of one of the signatories of the

Charter during World War II without authorisation by the Security Council.

Whether it has arisen through intention or neglect, it is time and in the interests of all Germans to ensure a sustained and founded clarification of the situation.

Community changeover

The constitutional principles of the FRG are set forth in Section 92(2) of the Criminal Code (StGB). The 1st constitutional principle states that the community/town councils and the mayor are the people's representatives, since they are elected "in a public, direct, free, equal and secret election." Exceptions are the German city states and certain parts of Schleswig-Holstein, where the mayors are not directly elected. In most of the federal states (except Baden-Württemberg and Schleswig Holstein) the Landräte [District Administrators] are also directly elected so that they are also representatives of the people.

i p. 167

The members of the federal and federal state parliaments are therefore not representatives of the people, since they are not elected in a direct manner. Likewise, the federal and federal state governments are not representatives of the people.

According to the 4th constitutional principle, however, the government is responsible towards the representatives of the people and it can and may be replaced.

Hence, every town and every community has the right to detach itself from the federal and federal state governments and then be fully autonomous or affiliate itself to another German government.

This also emerges from Art. 28 (2) of the Basic Law.

The communities have to be guaranteed the right to regulate all the affairs of the local community within their own responsibility and within the scope of the laws.

Every federal German state has local government laws as the legal foundation for the communities. In all these laws Section 1 states right at the beginning in various formulations and explanations that the communities constitute the foundation of the democratic state, that they promote the well-being of their citizens in free self-administration and that they have the right to administer local affairs within the scope of the laws. This last statement is an expression of the universally valid principle of subsidiarity.

i p. 163

The second statement shows that promotion of the well-being of the citizen is prescribed by law. So if a German citizen does not see their welfare being promoted, they can demand it from their representatives in the community or town council since in this case the community is not fulfilling its legal duty. If the people's representation dismisses these reproaches with references to constraints and duties through the federal state and federal governments, it violates the 4th constitutional principle pursuant to Section 92(2) of the Criminal Code (StGB). For it is not the people's representation that is responsible to the government but it is the government that is responsible to the people's representation. And if the government does not act in accordance with its responsibility, it can be replaced in accordance with the same constitutional principle.

If the people's representation (local council, mayor) is not able (or willing) to recognise and change this, the people has the right to elect a different people's representation or to exercise authority directly through ballot (1st constitutional principle). This happens through referendums, which are possible in all federal states. The citizens can also bring about a referendum if the community or town council does not cooperate. For this they just have to submit a sufficient number of signatures in favour of a referendum.

More details are regulated in the respective community regulations of the various federal states.

You can find further details and background information on the internet at

http://koenigreichdeutschland.org/de/gemeindewechsel.html

Public debts

On 31.12.2014 the debts of the towns and communities in Germany totalled approx. 150 bn euros [54].

At the same time, the private financial assets (cash and investments) of German households amounted to approx. 2000 bn euros [55].

Hence, only 7% of private assests on average would be sufficient to repay the debts of all towns and communities.

Therefore, if after a changeover every citizen of the town or community only changes 7% of their assets into Reichsmark at the Royal Reichsbank, the Reichsbank has sufficient euros to repay the debts of the town or community.

However, none of the citizens suffers a loss of purchasing power through this as they receive the equivalent value in Reichsmarks for the euros they change.

Glossary

BIS:	Abbreviation of "Bank for International Settlements"
FRG:	Abbreviation of "Federal Republic of Germany"
GDR:	Abbreviation of "German Democratic Republic"
Dun & Bradstreet:	Dun & Bradstreet is one of the largest suppliers of economic information worldwide. The firm keeps the world's largest economic database, which can be accessed at http://www.upik.de
Deposit protection fund:	Banks' system to protect their customers' money in the case of insolvency. The (German) statute of the deposit protection fund can be found on the internet at https://bankenverband.de/publikationen/statut-des-einlagensicherungsfonds/ (last accessed on 25.8.2015) Note especially Section 6, paragraph 10: *There is no legal right to intervention by or services from the deposit protection fund.*
ECB:	Abbreviation of "European Central Bank"
Fed:	Abbreviation of "Federal Reserve Bank"
Homeopathy:	Alternative medical treatment method going back to the German doctor Samuel Hahnemann. It is based on the principle of similarity in the choice of medical remedies ("Like be cured by like") and the principle of potentiation, through which the remedy does not work on account of its substance content but on account of its information content.
IPCC:	Intergovernmental Panel on Climate Change
Placebo:	A simulated or otherwise medically ineffectual treatment for a disease or other medical condition intended to deceive the recipient. (Source: Wikipedia, last accessed on 5.9.2015)

Ritalin:

Drug which has been used for some years for ADD (Attention Deficit Disorder/Hyperactivity Disorder). Ritalin works in principle like small doses of cocaine: it lowers the dopamine level in the nerve cells, thus suppressing the nerve impulses. This promotes focusing, i.e. virtually reduces the multidimensional functioning of the brain to one dimension. In other words, a human being becomes a robot.

Shetinin School:

An experimental school established in Russia in 1994 based on a novel pedagogical principle developed by Professor Michail Shetinin. The children organise almost all areas of their school life themselves and thus achieve a high universal level within a short time without external pressure.

Secession:

We speak of secession when part of an existing state detaches itself from this state in order to form its own sovereign state or join another state.

In a report by the International Court of Justice of 22.7.2010 [31] it is stated in IV.A that "general international law contains no applicable prohibition of declarations of independence."

WHO:

Abbreviation of "World Health Organization"

Sources

[1]   Königreich Deutschland (2014). Verfassung. Akasha Verlag
[2]   Bürgin, L. (2010). *Der Urzeit-Code.* Munich: Herbig
[3]   Paul, R. (16.9.2009). *End the Fed.* Grand Central Publishing
[4]   Gillens, M. & Page, B. I. (18.9.2014). *Testing Theories of American Politics: Elites, Interest Groups, and Average Citizens.* Perspectives on Politics Volume 12 / Issue 03 / September 2014, pp. 564-581. Last accessed on 5.9.2015 at http://dx.doi.org/10.1017/S1537592714001595
[5]   Marx, K. (1843). *Zur Kritik der Hegelschen Rechtsphilosophie.* Page 391
[6]   *Charta der Erneuerten Vereinten Nationen/Charter of the Renewed United Nations.* Last accessed on 25.9.2015 at http://www.united-nations.org
[7]   Hirte, M. (2012). *Impfen Pro & Contra.* München: Knaur
[8]   Humphries, S. & Bystrianyk, R. (2015). *Die Impf-Illusion.* Rottenburg: Kopp Verlag
[9]   Velikovsky, I. (1950). *Worlds in Collision.* Garden City, New York, USA: Doubleday & Company
[10] Velikovsky, I. (1955). *Earth in Upheaval.* Garden City, New York, USA: Doubleday & Company
[11] Velikovsky, I. (1982). *Mankind in Amnesia.* Garden City, New York, USA: Doubleday & Company
[12] Nahle, N. S. (5.7.2011). *Repeatability of Professor Robert W. Wood's 1909 experiment on the Theory of the Greenhouse.* Biology Cabinet Online-Academic Resources and Principia Scientific International. Monterrey, N. L.
      Last accessed on 5.9.2015 at http://www.biocab.org/Experiment_on_Greenhouses__Effect.pdf
[13] Ermecke, K. (Dez. 2009). *Rettung vor den Klimarettern – Gibt es die Gefahr für das Weltklima?* Last accessed on 5.9.2015 at http://www.ke-research.de/downloads/Klimaretter.pdf
[14] Gerlich,G. (28.11.2007). *Der Betrug mit dem Globalklima. Widerlegung der atmosphärischen Kohlendioxid-Treibhauseffekte der Erde.* Last accessed on 5.9.2015 at https://eppinger.files.wordpress.com/2009/12/der-betrug-mit-dem-globalklima.pdf

[15] Collection of Climategate I and II emails with search function. Last accessed on 5.9.2015 at http://www.ecowho.com/foia. php

[16] List of emails of [15] in an Excel spreadsheet. Last accessed on 5.9.2015 at https://noconsensus.files.wordpress. com/2011/11/odered-emails.xls

[17] D'Aleo, J. & Watts, A. (27.8.2010). *Surface temperature records: Policy-driven deception?* Science & Public Policy Institute. Last accessed on 5.9.2015 at http://scienceandpublicpolicy. org/images/stories/papers/originals/surface_temp.pdf

[18] Statistisches Bundesamt. (2014). *Finanzen und Steuern, Vierteljährliche Kassenergebnisse des öffentlichen Gesamthaushalts. 1. - 4. Vierteljahr 2013* (Fachserie 14, Reihe 2). Last accessed on 5.9.2015 at http://www.destatis.de/DE/Publikationen/Thematisch/FinanzenSteuern/ OeffentlicheHaushalte/AusgabenEinnahmen/ KassenergebnisOeffentlicherHaushalt2140200133244. pdf?__blob=publicationFile

[19] Statistisches Bundesamt. *Öffentliche Finanzen und Steuern.* Last accessed on 5.9.2015 at http://www.destatis.de/DE/ ZahlenFakten/Indikatoren/LangeReihen/SteuernFinanzen/ lrfin02.html

[20] Deutsche Bundesbank. (March 2015). *Die Ertragslage der deutschen Kreditinstitute.* Last accessed on 5.9.2015 at http://www.bundesbank.de/Redaktion/DE/Downloads/ Statistiken/Banken_Und_Andere_Finanzielle_Institute/ Banken/GuV_Statistik/guv_tab8.pdf?__blob=publicationFile

[21] Deutsche Bundesbank. (May 2015). *Hochgerechnete Angaben aus Jahresabschlüssen deutscher Unternehmen von 1997 bis 2013* (Statistische Sonderveröffentlichung 5). Last accessed on 5.9.2015 at http://www.bundesbank.de/ Redaktion/DE/Downloads/Veroeffentlichungen/Statistische_ Sonderveroeffentlichungen/Statso_5/statso5_1997_2013_ EXCEL.xlsb?__blob=publicationFile

[22] Bundesrechnungshof. (28.6.2010). *Bericht nach § 99 BHO über den ermäßigten Umsatzsteuersatz. Vorschläge für eine künftige Ausgestaltung der Steuerermäßigung.* Last accessed on 5.9.2015 at https://www.bundesrechnungshof.de/de/ veroeffentlichungen/sonderberichte/langfassungen/2010-sonderbericht-ermaessigter-umsatzsteuersatz-vorschlaege-fuer-

eine-kuenftige-ausgestaltung-der-steuerermaessigung

[23] Statistisches Bundesamt. (2012). *Finanzen und Steuern, Rechnungsergebnisse des öffentlichen Gesamthaushalts 2010* (Fachserie 14, Reihe 3.1). Last accessed on 5.9.2015 at http://www.destatis.de/DE/Publikationen/Thematisch/ F i n a n z e n S t e u e r n / O e f f e n t l i c h e H a u s h a l t e / AusgabenEinnahmen/RechnungsergebnisOeffentlicherHausha lt2140310107004.pdf?__blob=publicationFile

[24] Statistisches Bundesamt. (2014). *Finanzen und Steuern, Lohn- und Einkommensteuer 2010* (Fachserie 14, Reihe 7.1). Last accessed on 5.9.2015 at http://www.destatis. de/DE/Publikationen/Thematisch/FinanzenSteuern/ Steuern/LohnEinkommensteuer/LohnEinkommensteu er2140710109004.pdf?__blob=publicationFile

[25] Techniker Krankenkasse. (Januar 2013). *Beiträge ab 1. Januar 2013*. Last accessed on 5.9.2015 at http://www.tk.de/ centaurus/servlet/contentblob/491028/Datei/61478/ Beitragstabelle-2013.pdf

[26] Senf, B. (April 2011). *Und es gibt Sie doch! Die Geldschöpfung der Banken aus dem Nichts*. Last accessed on 5.9.2015 at http://www.wissensmanufaktur.net/media/pdf/Und sie gibt es doch Die Geldschoepfung der Banken aus dem Nichts.pdf

[27] Griffin, G. E. (4. 8. 2006). *Die Kreatur von Jekyll Island*. Rottenburg: Kopp Verlag.

[28] Jellinek, G. (1900). *Allgemeine Staatslehre*. Berlin: Haering

[29] *Montevideo Convention on the Rights and Duties of States.* (26.12.1933). Last accessed on 5.9.2015 at http://www.cfr. org/sovereignty/montevideo-convention-rights-duties-states/ p15897

[30] Pellet, A. (1992). *The Opinions of the Badinter Arbitration Committee. A Second Breath for the Self-Determination of Peoples*. Eur J Int Law (1992) 3 (1): 178-185. Last accessed on 5.9.2015 at http://ejil. o x f o r d j o u r n a l s . o r g / c o n t e n t / 3 / 1 / 1 7 8 . f u l l . pdf+html?sid=6c56ca2e-920d-41ed-b23c-57c4162ee897

[31] International Court of Justice (22. 7. 2010). *Accordance with international law of the unilateral declaration of independence in respect of Kosovo*. Summary 2010/2. Last accessed on 5.9.2015 at http://www.icj-cij.org/docket/ files/141/16010.pdf

[32] Nörr, K. W. & Oppermann, T. (Hrsg.). (1997). *Subsidiarität: Idee und Wirklichkeit*. Tübingen: Mohr.

[33] Foschepoth, J. (2014). *Überwachtes Deutschland*. Göttingen: Vandenhoeck & Ruprecht.

[34] *Vertrag über die Beziehungen zwischen der Bundesrepublik Deutschland und den Drei Mächten* (called "Deutschlandvertrag [Germany Agreement]"). (26.5.1952). Last accessed on 5.9.2015 at http://www.1000dokumente.de/index.html?c=dokument_de&dokument=0018_par&object=facsimile&pimage=18&v=100&nav=&l=de

[35] *Vertrag über die abschließende Regelung in bezug auf Deutschland* (called "Zwei-plus-Vier-Vertrag [Two Plus Four Treaty]"). (12.9.1990). Last accessed on 5.9.2015 at http://www.auswaertiges-amt.de/cae/servlet/contentblob/373162/publicationFile/3828/ZweiPlusVier%20(Text).pdf

[36] *Übereinkommen zur Regelung bestimmter Fragen in Bezug auf Berlin* (called "Berlin-Übereinkommen [Berlin Agreement]"). (25.9.1990). Last accessed on 5.9.2015 at http://www.auswaertiges-amt.de/cae/servlet/contentblob/576384/publicationFile/158728/VertragstextOriginal.pdf

[37] Auswärtiges Amt [Foreign Office]. *Endgültiges Erlöschen der alliierten Vorbehaltsrechte*. (31.5.1968) Page 1. Digital full-text edition at Wikisource. Last accessed on 5.9.2015 at https://de.wikisource.org/wiki/Seite:Endg%C3%BCltiges_Erl%C3%B6schen_der_alliierten_Vorbehaltsrechte.pdf/1

[38] *Bekanntmachung des Schreibens der Drei Mächte vom 8. Juni 1990 zur Aufhebung ihrer Vorbehalte insbesondere in dem Genehmigungsschreiben zum Grundgesetz vom 12. Mai 1949 in bezug auf die Direktwahl der Berliner Vertreter zum Bundestag und ihr volles Stimmrecht im Bundestag und im Bundesrat*. (12.6.1990). Last accessed on 5.9.2015 at http://www.gesetze-im-internet.de/bundesrecht/avorbaschrbek/gesamt.pdf

[39] *Vertrag über die Rechte und Pflichten ausländischer Streitkräfte und ihrer Mitglieder in der Bundesrepublik Deutschland*. (26.5.1952). Compilation of the Germany Agreement and its Additional Agreements — Bundesgesetzbl. [Federal Law Gazette] page 1954 II S.57 ff. — with the five lists of amendments to the Paris Protocol. Last accessed on 5.9.2015 at https://www.bundestag.de/blob/194030/028f8

b69d335f194759acc8467bdd099/deutschlanvertragzusamme nstellung-data.pdf

[40] *Zusatzabkommen zu dem Abkommen zwischen den Parteien des Nordatlantikvertrages über die Rechtsstellung ihrer Truppen hinsichtlich der in der Bundesrepublik Deutschland stationierten ausländischen Truppen.* (3.8.1959). Last accessed on 5.9.2015 at http://www.abg-plus.de/abg2/ebuecher/abg_ all/index.html

[41] *Vereinbarung vom 27./28.9.1990 zum Deutschlandvertrag und zum Überleitungsvertrag.* BGBl. [Federal Law Gazette] II page 1386. Last accessed on 5.9.2015 at http://www.ialana. de/files/pdf/arbeitsfelder/aktuell%20in%20der%20diskussion/ nsa-affaere/Zusatzvereinbarungen_zum_Deutschlandvertrag. pdf

[42] *Vereinbarung vom 25.9.1990 zum Aufenthaltsvertrag.* BGBl. II page 1390. Last accessed on 5.9.2015 at http://www.ialana. de/files/pdf/arbeitsfelder/aktuell%20in%20der%20diskussion/ nsa-affaere/Zusatzvereinbarungen_zum_Deutschlandvertrag. pdf

[43] *Vereinbarung vom 16.11.1990 zum Aufenthaltsvertrag.* BGBl. [Federal Law Gazette] II page 1696. Last accessed on 5.9.2015 at http://www.ialana.de/files/pdf/arbeitsfelder/aktuell%20 in%20der%20diskussion/nsa-affaere/Zusatzvereinbarungen_ zum_Deutschlandvertrag.pdf

[44] *Notenwechsel vom 25.9.1990 zum NATO-Truppenstatut und zum Truppenverbleib in Berlin.* BGBl. [Federal Law Gazette] II page 1251. Last accessed on 5.9.2015 at http://www.ialana. de/files/pdf/arbeitsfelder/aktuell%20in%20der%20diskussion/ nsa-affaere/Zusatzvereinbarungen_zum_Deutschlandvertrag. pdf

[45] *Denkschrift zum Notenwechsel vom 25.9.1990.* BR-Drucks. 357/90 page. 13ff. Last accessed on 5.9.2015 at http://www.ialana.de/files/pdf/arbeitsfelder/aktuell%20 in%20der%20diskussion/nsa-affaere/Zusatzvereinbarungen_ zum_Deutschlandvertrag.pdf

[46] *Vertrag zur Regelung aus Krieg und Besatzung entstandener Fragen* (called "Überleitungsvertrag [Transition Treaty]"). (26.5.1952). Last accessed on 5.9.2015 at https://www. bundestag.de/blob/194030/028f8b69d335f194759acc8467 bdd099/deutschlanvertragzusammenstellung-data.pdf

[47]   Bahr, E. (8.9.2009). *Drei Briefe und ein Staatsgeheimnis*. Die Zeit N° 21/2009. Last accessed on 5.9.2015 at http://www. zeit.de/2009/21/D-Souveraenitaet

[48]   documentArchiv.de (publisher). *Erklärung in Anbetracht der Niederlage Deutschlands und der Übernahme der obersten Regierungsgewalt hinsichtlich Deutschlands durch die Regierungen des Vereinigten Königreichs, der Vereinigten Staaten von Amerika und der Union der Sozialistischen Sowjet-Republiken und durch die Provisorische Regierung der Französischen Republik*. (5.6.1945). Last accessed on 5.9.2015 at http://www.documentarchiv.de/in/1945/ niederlage-deutschlands_erkl.html

[49]   *Abkommen betreffend die Gesetze und Gebräuche des Landkriegs* (called "Haager Landkriegsordnung [Hague Convention Respecting the Rules of War on Land]"). (18.10.1907). Last accessed on 5.9.2015 at http://www.1000dokumente.de/ index.html?c=dokument_de&dokument=0201_haa& object=pdf&l=de

[50]   *Dokumente zur künftigen politischen Entwicklung Deutschlands* (called "Frankfurter Dokumente [Frankfurt Documents]"). (1.7.1948). Last accessed on 5.9.2015 at http://www.1000dokumente.de/index.html?c= dokument_de&dokument=0012_fra&object=facsimile& pimage=1&v=100&nav=&l=de

[51]   Krämer, J. D. *Gesamtstaatliche Aspekte der Rittersturzkonferenz 1948*. Deutscher Bundestag Wissenschaftliche Dienste WD 1 - 3010 - 038/08. Last accessed on 5.9.2015 at http:// w e b a r c h i v . b u n d e s t a g . d e / c g i / s h o w . php?fileToLoad=4082&id=1081

[52]   *Vertrag zwischen der Bundesrepublik Deutschland und der Deutschen Demokratischen Republik über die Herstellung der Einheit Deutschlands* (called "Einigungsvertrag [Unification Treaty]"). (31.8.1990). BGBl. [Federal Law Gazette] II 1990 page 889. Last accessed on 5.9.2015 at http://www.gesetze-im-internet.de/bundesrecht/einigvtr/gesamt.pdf

[53]   Küsters, H. J. & Hofmann, D. (1998). *Dokumente zur Deutschlandpolitik. Deutsche Einheit: Sonderedition aus den Akten des Bundeskanzleramtes 1989/90*. B 136-ANH./8 No. 354 B Annexe 2: Minutes of the French chairman. Münich: Oldenbourg

[54] Statistisches Bundesamt. *Schulden des Öffentlichen Gesamthaushalts am 31.12.2014 beim nicht-öffentlichen Bereich.* Last accessed on 23.11.2015 at http://www.destatis.de/DE/ZahlenFakten/GesellschaftStaat/OeffentlicheFinanzenSteuern/OeffentlicheFinanzen/Schulden/Tabellen/SchuldenOeffentlHaushalte_2014.html

[55] Deutsche Bundesbank. *Financial assets and liabilities (non-consolidatet).* Last accessed on 23.11.2015 at http://www.bundesbank.de/Redaktion/EN/Pressemitteilungen/BBK/2015/2015_07_20_table_financial_assets_and_liabilities_non_consolidated.pdf?__blob=publicationFile

The author

After his studies of mathematics, physics and other natural sciences in Germany and the USA, Dr. Hoffmann did a PhD in applied mathematics and has since been occupying himself intensively with concrete applications of natural laws in human life.

www.ingramcontent.com/pod-product-compliance
Lightning Source LLC
Chambersburg PA
CBHW031201270326
41931CB00006B/359